By their own Hand

By their own Hand

suicides by the rich and famous

by

David Lester

Aeneas

First Published 2000
by AENEAS Press

PO BOX 200
Chichester PO 18 OYX
West Sussex.
United Kingdom

Typeset in Times New Roman

Printed and Bound by MPG Books
Bodmin, Cornwall
United Kingdom

ISBN: 1- 902115- 09- 0

British Library Cataloging in Publication Data
A catalogue record of this book is available from the British Library
Lester, David.

Contents

1. BRIAN EPSTEIN:

THE MAN WHO MADE THE BEATLES

Queenie Hyman and Harry Epstein met while they were on holiday. They fell in love and were married in September, 1933. She was eighteen, he was twenty-nine. Both came from Jewish families which ran successful businesses: Queenie's father made furniture, and Harry's father sold furniture. The couple moved to a newly built house in the suburbs of Liverpool after the wedding, and Harry worked in his father's store. Queenie kept a kosher home, and they observed the religious festivals and ceremonies.

Their first son, Brian, was born on September 19, 1934, The parents hired a live-in nanny when Brian was six months old. He was a determined child, spotless in hygiene, and rarely cried. Brian had a squint corrected when he was five, but it reappeared when he was under stress.

Brian decided that he wanted to become a dress designer, but his father disapproved, and so Brian quit school at the age of sixteen to work in the furniture store. He was a good salesman, and he began to show an aptitude for running a store successfully. By the age of eighteen he was an affluent and debonair bachelor. His father decided to expand his store to include records, and he put Brian in charge. The store became a profitable success within a year.

At this time, Brian was, on the surface, a fine young man — generous, well-dressed, with an interest in horse racing and tennis. He took suitably nice holidays and was seen with female companions. He was, however, a shy man and uneasy in social gatherings. He had many acquaintances, but few close friends. He was also homosexual and, when he finally told his parents, they were understanding.

1

After a year in acting school, he decided against acting as a career and returned to his father's stores. As a result of running successful record stores, Brian got involved with the world of pop music. He attended concerts, met the artists and their promoters, and broadened his awareness of the music scene in Liverpool. At this time there were several hundred groups in the area performing at the local clubs. Eventually, he noticed the Beatles. Their German records sold well in his stores, and he read about them in the local popular music paper. Finally, he had a chance to see them at Cavern, one of the Liverpool clubs, and he thought that they were incredible. There and then he decided to be their manager.

The history of Brian Epstein soon became inextricably bound up in the fortunes of the Beatles. They agreed to let him manage them and signed with him on February 1, 1962, for a five year period. Brian loved the Beatles, and they became his obsession, his alter ego, and his triumph, for, despite the fact that they were, of course, incredibly talented, it was Brian who shaped their image, fought for the first record contracts, and truly advanced their career.

But several themes developed in the years leading up to Brian's suicide. First, he began using drugs. Brian had always drank heavily, so much that friends and acquaintances commented on it. He soon began to smoke marihuana heavily, took LSD, experimented with heroin, and became hooked on uppers and downers (amphetamines and barbiturates) — though the psychiatrist who treated him in the months before his death did not consider him addicted! Brian had special inside pockets sown in his clothes for his supply of amphetamines. The effect on his behavior was tremendous. Staff and friends observed tremendous mood swings, profound depressions, and outbursts of anger. At times, he could barely function for days at a time, and his staff would have to cancel appointments and cover for him.

His death, on August 27, 1967, was due to an overdose of the medication his psychiatrist had prescribed for him, Carbitral, which contains pentobarbitone and bromide. He was supposed to be taking two Carbitral tablets a night on his psychiatrist's order, as well as Tryptizol and Librium. The coroner ruled the death an accidental poisoning caused by an incautious overdose. Some acquaintances believed that his death was accidental, perhaps a case of "drug automatism" in which the person forgets how many pills he has taken, keeps taking more and overdoses by mistake. However, experts in the field of suicide have never documented a case in which drug automatism has been shown to be a real phenomenon!

Although the Beatles were the major focus of his life, Brian had to endure much stress from them. They mocked his style and his mannerisms and insulted his religion and his sexual orientation. John Lennon, in particular, was especially cruel to Brian, as indeed he was to many of his friends. He sang "Baby, you're a rich fag Jew" to Brian and once, when Ringo damaged a chair at Brian's house and Brian tried to prevent it, John said that Ringo had paid for it so he could destroy it. Yet Brian seems never to have retaliated. He endured the abuse and walked away, believing that the Beatles were geniuses and that it was the price one had to pay to be with them.

In time, the Beatles began to be independent. George questioned Brian's business dealings, and the Beatles began to talk of setting up their own companies. After their American tour in 1966, they decided never to tour again, a decision which would have drastically reduced Brian's role in their lives. Brian's contract to manage the Beatles was due to be renegotiated in September, 1967, and it was likely to be terminated. He killed himself one month before the contract expired!

Brian was not at ease with his homosexuality. He tried to date women, even to the point of sexual intimacy, and he made a serious proposal of marriage to one. He regretted that he was not married with a family. Brian was not attracted to homosexuals. He liked masculine heterosexual types, and as a result his overtures to the men he liked best were usually rejected. He had one or two brief relationships with gay men which might have become more permanent, but he typically broke these relationships off after a month or two.

He worried a great deal that public disclosure of his homosexuality might endanger the career of the Beatles. In fact, he was petrified of being revealed publicly as a homosexual. After he had moved into his London house, someone gouged the word queer on his car and painted the word on his garage door.

Finally, his success with the Beatles led him to overextend his management empire. He took on many artists, but he did not really have the time to work for them effectively, especially since he was abusing drugs. Yet he also was reluctant to delegate responsibility to his staff, so that his artists' careers suffered. After the success with the Beatles, his first group, Brian was not used to failure. By the year of his death, Brian was managing forty musicians, had eighty staff, and was directly involved in sixty-five registered companies! He was working seven days a week, day and night, often sleeping only two hours a night.

During his last five years, Brian's psychological state became increasingly worse. When the Beatles were honored by the Queen in 1965, Brian was not, and he fell into a depression. He had been depressed many times in his life. He had seen three psychiatrists in the two years prior to his death. In May 1967, Brian was hospitalized by a psychiatrist for three weeks for a "complete rest". He was reported to have been suffering from insomnia, anxiety and depression. Immediately on his release, he threw a huge LSD party at his country home!

On the weekend of his death, he had planned to go to his country home with two friends, and he had invited others to join them. On Friday evening, he was bored by his two friends and disappointed that no one else had arrived, so he left his friends and drove back to London. On Saturday, his servants served him an evening meal at five. After that he locked his door. On Sunday afternoon he was still not responding, so his servants called his secretary who went over and called a doctor. They found him dead when they broke down his bedroom door.

Although some question whether Brian's death as a suicide, most of those close to Brian expected a tragic ending to his life. His mother thought something was amiss when he was unavailable to come to the telephone during that weekend, and several of his friends anticipated that Brian might one day commit suicide. It seems that they were correct.

2. ALAN TURING:

THE INVENTOR OF COMPUTERS

Alan Turing was a very eccentric Englishman who invented the idea of the computer before anyone had ever built one or even thought of building one. These "hypothetical" machines were known as "Turing Machines."

Turing's father worked in the Indian Civil Service, and his mother was born in India, the daughter of an Anglo-Irish Major in the Indian Army. Alan, their second child, was born in England on June 23, 1912. Their father returned to India, but their mother stayed until September, 1913. She then left for India leaving the two children with a retired Army couple near Hastings in England, by the English Channel, until she returned in 1916.

Alan was a precocious child, with a high-pitched voice, naughty and willful, and prone to throw temper tantrums when he could not get his own way. Although he displayed initiative and creativity early on, he had problems in school where Latin was difficult for him to learn, and he had trouble writing.

His mother left for India again in 1921 and, when she returned, Alan's school work was very poor. He could not do even long-division, and he had changed from being extremely vivacious, mercurial and sociable to being unsociable, dreamy, wistful and withdrawn. In early 1922 Alan was sent off to boarding school.

School was a trial for Alan (and his teachers). Alan was obviously very bright. However, the things he liked to do, for example, paper folding and studying maps as a child, mathematics problems and science experiments later, were never what his teachers wanted him to do. When forced to participate in the authorized activities, he was untidy, unmotivated, and performed poorly. Alan was nicknamed dirty because of his dark, greasy complexion; his pens leaked, and he was always covered with ink stains; his hair refused to lie down, and his shirt never tucked in his trousers; his voice was high-pitched, and he was shy and hesitant.

However, by the time he entered the Sixth Form (roughly corresponding to eleventh grade), Alan was recognized as a math brain at the school. In the Sixth Form, he finally made a close friend, Christopher Morcom, who shared his interest in science. Alan was aware of his sexual attraction to other boys by the age of fifteen, and Christopher was probably Alan's first love.

Christopher died unexpectedly in February, 1930, as a consequence of contracting tuberculosis from drinking milk many years earlier. Alan was hit hard by this loss, and Christopher remained an important figure in his life for many years. He became close to Christopher's parents, almost a surrogate son to them, and he never failed to remember Christopher's birthday and deathday.

At his second try, Alan was awarded a scholarship by his second choice, King's College, Cambridge University, and he decided to read mathematics there. It is odd that Alan, on the path to becoming a homosexual, should have arrived almost by chance at the college with the reputation of being the college for homosexuals (based on the fair number of distinguished homosexuals who had been students and fellows there). Surprisingly, Alan remained distant from the homosexual cliques at King's.

Alan passed Part Two of his degree with distinction in 1934, and a year later he was elected a fellow at the college, a three year position which could be extended to six years, with no explicit duties. Alan had been interested for a long time in the idea of an electrical brain, a computing machine that would carry out logical operations. In a now classic paper, "On Computable Numbers" published in the Proceedings of the London Mathematical Society, he set up a hypothetical model, a new framework for thinking about computing, which later became known as a Turing Machine.

After a brief stay at Princeton University in America, where he obtained a Ph.D. degree, Alan returned to England to join the British Government's efforts to break the German communication codes during the War. He not only helped breaking the German codes, but also to help design machines to speed up the work involved, and he was honored by the King after the war for his work.

Alan was quite eccentric in his personal style. For example, during the war, he suffered from hay fever, so he would cycle to work wearing a gas mask. His trousers were held up by string or a tie, and he often wore a pyjama jacket under his sports coat, which itself had holes. His hair stuck out at the back. He hated shaving so that he had a permanent five o'clock shadow, and he passed out at the sight of blood, even his own. His teeth were yellow though he did not smoke. His hands were usually dirty with scabs from where he picked at them. He tended not to greet people, finding saying hello all the time "redundant." His manner was nervous, and his voice would often stall in mid-sentence with a tense, high-pitched "ah-ah-ah-ah" while he sought for a word. He had a machine-like laugh. 'Schoolboyish' described him, though his nickname was 'Prof.'

After the war, in 1948, he joined the staff at Manchester University whose staff were also constructing a computer. However, although he helped the development of the computers there and used them to solve his own problems, he began to lose interest in computer development. His interests switched to embryology, and he published an innovative paper on this in 1952 in the Philosophical Transactions of the Royal Society. He was elected a Fellow of the Royal Society in 1951, one of the youngest to be elected.

In 1950, he finally bought himself a house, ending his days of landladies and suitcases. He got on well with his neighbors who seemed unperturbed by Alan's eccentricities. He had a woman shop and clean for him, though he did make an effort to develop some domestic skills.

Alan, though he had by now experienced a couple of long-term homosexual relationships, began to look for casual pick-ups. One of these was Arnold Murray, an unemployed nineteen year-old with a criminal record for theft. Arnold visited Alan several times, borrowing money from Alan. On January 23, 1952, Alan found that his house had been burglarized, and he reported it to the police. He suspected Arnold and, when confronted, Arnold admitted that it had probably been a friend of his. Alan gave the police information about the thief but tried to hide his source of information. When detectives came to interview him, he blurted out that fact of his affair with Arnold.

At this time, homosexuality was a crime in England. The police now changed their opinion of the 'crime,' ignored the burglary, and charged Alan instead with homosexual offenses. Alan informed his relatives and friends so that they would not be shocked, and his brother persuaded him to plead guilty so as to minimize the publicity. Alan's close friends knew of his homosexuality, Manchester University colleagues viewed the matter as one more Turing eccentricity, and his family accepted the matter calmly. Alan was placed on probation on the condition he receive treatment involving injections with estrogen. Alan accepted the effects on his body (impotence and the development of bodily changes, such as breasts) in order that he could remain free to pursue his intellectual work. However, Alan did enter into long-term psychotherapy with a Jungian analyst, and he achieved some insights through this. Alan now travelled in order to find homosexual partners, taking holidays in Norway, France and Corfu, where he found casual relationships.

Alan was promoted at the University in May 1953, but a year later, on June 7, 1954, he killed himself. His suicide came as a shock to those who knew Alan. There was no warning and no note of explanation. His trial was two years in the past, and the hormone treatments had ended. He was as active as ever in his research, perhaps in an interregnum between topics, but he had weathered such periods before.

Alan was found on the morning of Tuesday, June 8, by his housekeeper. He was lying neatly in bed, with froth around his mouth, and the postmortem identified cyanide as the cause of his death. By the side of his bed was a half-eaten apple which was never analyzed. Alan's mother believed that her son's death was an accident, that some of the nasty chemicals that Alan often experimented with had somehow been ingested. But the coroner's verdict was suicide.

If Alan's traumatic experience with being homosexual did indeed contribute to his decision to kill himself, he need only to have waited. In the early 1960s, homosexual behavior between consenting adults was decriminalized in England.

3. SOCRATES: THE GREEK PHILOSOPHER

WHO CARRIED OUT

HIS OWN EXECUTION

Socrates was the son of Sophroniscus and Phaenarete from Alopeke, a town on the road from Athens to the marble quarries of Pentelicon. He was born in 470 or 469 B.C. He was executed in 399 at the age of seventy.

His father has been described as a stonemason and as a sculptor, and Socrates may have learned the craft as a youth before he became a philosopher/teacher. His mother was perhaps a midwife. As a young man, he participated in the Peloponnesian War between Sparta and Athens which was eventually won by Sparta. He was obviously noteworthy in Athens since Aristophanes and Ameipsias both made him the subject of comedies in 423.

He next appears in the record in 406 when it was his turn to participate in the Council of Five Hundred, and he argued against trying the generals at the battle of Arginusae as a group — such a trial was in fact illegal under Athenian law.

He married late in life to Xanthippe, by whom he had three sons, one still an infant when Socrates died. His wife has been described as a shrew, but some commentators have suggested it was far from easy being the wife of an old philosopher who earned no money and appeared rather indifferent to his family. (Socrates apparently lived on income from a small inheritance from his father.)

Socrates was apparently quite ugly, with a broad, flat, turned-up nose, prominent staring eyes, thick fleshy lips, and a paunch. He regularly went about barefoot, wearing an old coat, and unwashed. He was considered to have excellent self-control. He was never drunk, and he kept his appetite for food and sex under strict control.

Socrates was put on trial in 399, found guilty and sentenced to death. The traditional death sentence in Athens was to drink hemlock, but what makes Socrates' death suicide was not simply his acquiescence to the death sentence, but the fact that he could easily have escaped a guilty verdict and the death sentence. He sought to be executed, and this is what makes his death truly suicidal!

Athens was a fully participatory democracy with freedom of speech as one its main tenets. As a result, Athens attracted thinkers from all over who came there to exchange ideas and to debate one another. Socrates was one of the leading philosophers there, but his views were rather odd. First, Socrates was completely opposed to democracy. He favored authoritarian rule by experts. Just as shoemakers must know how to make shoes, rulers must know how to rule. Only those who have the correct knowledge should be allowed to rule. Then the ruler orders, and the ruled must obey. Clearly, Socrates and his followers were out of step with the Athenians.

Did Socrates threaten the leaders of Athens? Socrates used his wisdom to make the leaders appear to be ignorant fools and, by his tactics, he turned some of the young men of the city against the democracy and encouraged them to disdain even the common people of Athens. However, the playwrights frequently did this in their plays, and they were not censored, so this in itself is not sufficient cause for the trial of Socrates.

Athens was based on participation by all in the government of the city, while Socrates preached withdrawal from political life. For himself, in seventy years, he hardly participated. Although he did not participate in movements which overthrew the democracy, neither did he participate in the restoration of democracy.

Important for understanding the reasons for his trial and conviction was the fact that two of his students helped overthrow the democratic government in Athens. Part of the charge against Socrates was that he led the youth to despise the established constitution and made them violent. In 411 the overthrow of the government was led by Alcibiades after which followed a period of rule by the Four Hundred. In 404, a group of thirty overthrew the government, aided by Sparta which had defeated Athens in the Peloponnesian War.

The rule of the Four Hundred lasted only four months and the rule of Thirty only eight months, but there were many horrors committed during those brief periods. The possibility of new horrors must have scared the Athenians so much that now Socrates's ideas were seen as very dangerous. In both coups, the aristocracy joined with the middle classes to disfranchise the lower classes, and then the aristocracy turned against the middle class. The aristocracy proved to be cruel, rapacious and bloody. The Thirty killed more than fifteen hundred Athenians in eight months, more than had died in the last decade of the Peloponnesian War.

Although there was an amnesty after the coup of 404, some of the Thirty refused to be reconciled and moved to the nearby town of Eleusis. The Athenians learned that the leaders of Eleusis were planning to attack Athens in 401 and attacked first and defeated them. Thus, Athens in 399 had much to fear from the followers of Socrates, and so they tried him.

The vote for Socrates' guilt was probably 280 guilty and 220 for acquittal. Socrates was surprised that so many voted for acquittal for, according to Xenophon, he did his best to antagonize the jury, particularly by being boastful and arrogant. It seemed as if seventy years of life was enough for Socrates, and he was worried about becoming frail and losing his hearing and vision. He acknowledged that trial and execution was a way to commit suicide. We call this now a victim-precipitated homicide, because the victim acts in such a way as to force (or encourage) others kill him.

Next came the vote for the penalty. Athenian juries could vote only for the penalty proposed by the prosecution or that proposed by the accused. The prosecution demanded the death penalty. Socrates offered first that he should be fed free of charge for the rest of his life as a civic hero. He next offered a fine of one mina, a trivial amount but, following pressure from Plato and other followers, suggested thirty minas of silver. The jury voted for the death penalty by a vote of about 360 to 140.

A proposal of banishment from the city or a reasonable fine would have pleased the jury. He probably could have won acquittal by appealing to the Athenian commitment to free speech. But for Socrates to appeal to the Athenian system would have given the system a moral victory over him.

After the verdict, when Socrates was in prison, his followers arranged for his escape. Socrates refused. He said it was his duty to obey the court's verdict and die. So Socrates drank the hemlock and died and, in doing so, fulfilled his own death wish.

4. LEICESTER HEMINGWAY:

ERNEST'S YOUNGER BROTHER

Ernest Hall was born in 1840 in Britain, came to the United States as a teenager and fought in the Civil War. Later, he made money in the cutlery business in Chicago. In 1905 he was dying and suffering from severe pain. He was planning to kill himself with a gun that he kept under his pillow. His son-in-law removed the bullets, and he tried to shoot himself with the unloaded gun.

His son-in-law was Ed Hemingway, a doctor. In 1928 Ed Hemingway suffered a financial loss from properties he had bought in Florida, and he found out that he had diabetes which he had failed to diagnose and treat. He suffered from terrible headaches, hardening of the arteries and angina pectoris. He feared gangrene of his feet, a result of the untreated diabetes, which might have necessitated amputation. Ed Hemingway shot himself in his bedroom one lunchtime with a .32 Smith and Wesson revolver that had been used by his father, Anson Hemingway, in the Civil War.

Ed Hemingway had six children. Ursula Hemingway Jepson developed cancer and underwent three operations. She was depressed, and in 1966 she killed herself with an overdose of drugs. The suicide of Ed Hemingway's oldest son, Ernest Hemingway is well known. The youngest child, Leicester, was born in 1915, in Oak Park, Illinois. Leicester was home in bed with flu on the day his father came home at lunch and shot himself. Leicester, only thirteen years old, discovered the body. Leicester shot himself on September 13, 1982, in Miami Beach, Florida.

Leicester notes that he was unplanned. He was looked after by his five older siblings, and even Ernest changed his diapers sometimes. Leicester learnt to hunt and fish both from his father and from Ernest. Leicester was sixteen years younger than Ernest and did not get to know his older brother well until the 1930s. He spent a great deal of effort imitating and trying to win the favor of his older brother, but eventually (in the 1940s) Ernest rejected him. Leicester remembers Ernest coming home from the First World War as a hero, and he remembers idolizing him. Leicester went to Ernest's high school and wrote for the same school newspaper (The Trapeze). Ernest encouraged Leicester to be a writer and advised him to work in journalism as he himself had done.

Leicester had similar looks to Ernest, but inherited his mother's blue eyes and blond hair. Ernest said that he always disliked Leicester because Leicester reminded him of his mother. He was also embarrassed by Leicester's enthusiasm and ineptitude and the failure of almost all his endeavors. Leicester wrecked a boat he had built when he sailed it to Cuba in 1934. He tried to be a sportsman, tough guy, and writer but never equalled Ernest. (Of course, had he ever equalled Ernest, Ernest would have been extremely jealous!) Ernest also felt that Leicester traded on Ernest's reputation and was a bore and a nuisance.

In 1936, Leicester married an adopted daughter of his Uncle Tyler, and they had two sons (Peter and Jake). He built boats, worked for the USIS in Bogota, went into the shrimp business, declared himself king of a tiny Caribbean island, was a bookmaker and a publicity man for a jai alai fronton in Miami, ran a charter boat in Montego Bay, and wrote adventure stories for a magazine in New York City. He published a war novel (The Sound of Trumpets) in 1953, which Ernest considered to be quite poor. Later, Ernest burnt one of Leicester's manuscripts without telling him.

Leicester spent time with his brother during the

years in Cuba in the 1930s, joining in his fishing and drinking adventures. In those days Ernest liked to have a kid brother around, someone to whom he could show off, someone to teach, someone to admire him. Leicester himself noted that his worshipful awe of Ernest eased the relationship with his brother. For a while, Leicester filled the role of junior crony, obliging confidant and trusted playmate.

Leicester continued to imitate his brother after Ernest's death. He grew a beard and began to resemble him physically. For the last five years of his life, he published a small monthly newsletter on fishing (The Bimini Out Islands News), living with his second wife Doris and his two daughters (Ann and Hilary). He developed severe diabetes and had five operations. Threatened with loss of his limbs he became depressed. He shot himself in the head with a borrowed handgun.

Leicester's life seemed to be an imitation of his brother's, but much less successful in the view of commentators. Leicester was not judged to be as good a novelist or journalist. He was a mere side note in biographies of Ernest. The New York Times indexed his death under Ernest's name, and his suicide was seen as Leicester imitating Ernest once again.

When I first wrote about Leicester Hemingway's suicide, I called my article "Living in the Shadow." Later, his daughter sent me a movie script she had written about her father, called "The Light in the Shadow." We saw his life in the same way!

5. ARSHILE GORKY: A PAINTER WHO SURVIVED THE ARMENIAN GENOCIDE

Arshile Gorky was an Armenian, born in 1904, who, after his emigration to the United States in 1920, became a well-regarded artist. He committed suicide at his home in Connecticut in 1948. What is sad about his life is that he survived so much hardship as a child and yet succumbed to despair after suffering misfortunes as an adult. Rather than preparing him to cope with whatever stress life presented him, the trauma of his childhood seems to have led him to conclude that he could not, or would not, endure such trauma again.

Gorky was born on April 15, 1904, as Visdanik Adoian in the village of Khorkum on the south shore of Lake Van in what is now eastern Turkey. From an early age he showed an interest in art. He was carving wood and sculpting clay at the age of four and drawing at the age of five. Friends from those days recall Gorky painting beautiful pictures on raven's eggs, carving flutes out of wood and molding animals out of clay.

His father left for America when Gorky was four, leaving his family behind. In 1909, Turkish troops began to massacre the Armenians, and in 1914 the Turkish forces laid siege to Van. On June 15 1915, Gorky's family began the journey to Caucasian Armenia (in what became the USSR), and they arrived in Yerevan on July 16. Gorky's sister has related how they walked day and night, with little food and with little rest, and how they survived epidemics of cholera.

By the end of 1915, the war with Turkey had led to the death of more than two million Armenians, almost three quarters of the entire nation. Gorky's two older sisters (Akabi and Satenik) left for the United States in October 1916 leaving Gorky and his younger sister,

Vartoosh, with their mother. In 1918, the family was living in an abandoned roofless room in a war-torn sector of Yerevan. Gorky's mother became very sick, primarily from lack of food, but the hospital would not admit her since she had a husband in America who presumably was sending her money. Gorky's sister says that no money ever arrived from her father. On March 20, 1919, Gorky's mother died in the arms of her two children. She was 39. Gorky was 15 and his sister was 13.

At the end of the year, their father sent money to pay for their passage to America, and so the children left for Constantinople from where they travelled to Athens, eventually getting on board a ship bound for America on February 9, 1920. They arrived at Ellis Island on February 26 and were with their older sister in Watertown, Massachusetts, by March 1. Gorky saw his father in Providence for the first time in twelve years.

Gorky attended school in Providence and decided to pursue a career in art. He moved to New York City and found a studio on Washington Square. At this time he adopted the name Arshile Gorky, primarily it seems because he was not confident of the quality of his art. He planned to use this pseudonym until his skills were perfected, after which he planned to revert back to his Armenian name. He told his sister that he did not want to bring shame on his people and that he would reveal his true identity only when he became famous. Yet all of those who knew Gorky in America say that he was proud of being Armenian. He told tales of life in Armenia, sang Armenian songs and danced to them when drunk, and dreamed of returning to Armenia to live.

From 1926 to 1931, Gorky taught at the Grand Central School of Art, and students remember him as knowledgeable about art and as a good teacher. He continued to paint and develop his style, and his first one-man show was at the Mellon Gallery in

Philadelphia in 1934. However, as with many artists during this period, Gorky was never financially secure, and he was usually short of money. He spent what little he had on art supplies and books. Friends and acquaintances recalled what a fine collection of brushes and what a large quantity of paint he had in his studio, but he neglected his diet in order to buy all of this. His sister sent him money and food whenever she could to help him survive. (Times were really hard then. One of Gorky's artist friends died of malnutrition in 1936.) Friends remember him as being intense, an exciting teacher, six feet four inches tall, with a moustache and black hair. He dressed elegantly and had a dark Armenian look and messianic force. One friend related that he would go into Italian neighborhoods, calling the young men "Wops," simply to provoke physical fights for exercise.

Gorky briefly married and divorced an American, Marney George in 1935. He married another American, Agnes Magruder, in 1941, with whom he had two daughters, Maro born April 5, 1943, and Natasha born August 8, 1945. Though he loved his daughters dearly, he also complained to friends that having a wife and babies in his studio made work difficult. This prompted his move out of New York to Connecticut where he could find more space.

In 1946 Gorky was diagnosed as having cancer and had several operations. He had a colostomy and had to wear a colostomy bag. He had to wash carefully and watch his diet. In the same year, a fire destroyed his studio in Connecticut along with all of his work. Friends recall Gorky banging his head on the ground saying that his whole life's work had been destroyed and that he had lost everything.

On June 26, 1948, he was a passenger in a car driven by his art dealer, Julian Levy, which crashed, and he suffered a broken neck and a temporarily paralyzed painting arm. He had to wear a neck collar, and he was afraid that he might never be able to paint again. In July, 1948, his wife left him, taking the two children. He was very depressed, and his friends worried that he might kill himself. On July 21, they found that he had hung himself, leaving a note scrawled in chalk on a wooden picture crate, "Goodbye My Loveds."

Gorky never felt at home in America. Despite the fact he took citizenship in May, 1939, he always despised America and longed to go home to Armenia. He felt that Americans did not understand or appreciate his art — "Nineteen miserable years have I lived in America," he would say. However, he never did return. This is surprising since his sister and her husband did return in the 1930s.

Most of those who knew Gorky remembered him as a melancholy person, and his nephew says that Gorky's mother was the same. He swung from feelings of despair about his work to feelings that he was a great artist.

Gorky once said that "his friends had to put up with Gorky once in while, but Gorky had to put up with himself all the time".

6. KONOE FUMIMARO: THE JAPANESE PRIME MINISTER WHO OPPOSED THE WAR

Konoe Fumimaro was born on October 12, 1891, to a noble family. His mother died eight days after his birth from puerperal fever, and his father married his wife's sister the following year. Konoe grew up thinking that this second wife was his mother, and it was a shattering blow when he later learned that she was not his biological mother. He grew up with a younger stepsister and three younger stepbrothers.

Konoe's father died at the age of 40 in 1904 when Konoe was twelve, and the family's fortunes changed. His family was aristocratic, one of the five elite families of the nation. Konoe himself was introduced to the Imperial household when he was two. Konoe's father had become involved with politics, developed a reputation as a nationalist, and was considered a possible future prime minister. After his death, friends and acquaintances wanted his debts paid, and the family had to sell off heirlooms to pay these debts. Konoe developed a distrust of people from this experience and from the deceit about his real mother.

Konoe inherited the title of Prince from his father, and the household now addressed him as Lord. Though he was a good runner, his guardian refused to let him participate in athletics at high school since he was a prince. Classmates remembered him as aloof and full of aristocratic airs, but his demeanor was partly the result of his distrust of others. He later described himself as a melancholy and jaundiced youth. He developed an antagonism toward the privileged class and considered giving up his title and becoming a professor of philosophy.

Konoe entered the Department of Philosophy at Tokyo Imperial University in 1912, but he switched to law at Kyoto Imperial University. In 1913 he married for love rather than through an arrangement, but he purchased a geisha as his mistress soon after marrying. He was a rather radical student, translating Oscar Wilde's essay, "The soul of man under socialism", which resulted in the issues of journal which had published it being banned. He graduated in 1918 just as the First World War was ending.

Konoe's political career developed quickly. In 1919, Konoe was part of the Japanese delegation to the Paris peace conference. After the conference, he travelled to Germany, England and the United States, and his experiences led him to question traditional Japanese customs and ceremonies.

His title gave him an automatic seat in the House of Peers. In 1921, he was elected acting president. Initially he joined a powerful faction in the house, the Kenkyukai, which had a reputation for corruption, and he was soon elected to the standing committee of this faction. Now, his father's old friends, who had turned against the family, began to return to the fold of this rising political star, thereby increasing Konoe's distrust of them.

In 1931, the first of several attempted coups by young military officers occurred. At this point, some of his political friends convinced him of the trivia of the party politics of the House of Peers. There were more serious issues. Konoe began to develop contacts with the military, especially the right-wing activists, and to learn of their views. In 1932, Japan declared Manchuria to be an independent state called Manchukuo under their rule. There followed another attempted coup and the assassination of a former minister of the government. Konoe vigorously defended Japan's advance into Manchuria and Mongolia, which earned him the support of the military and right-wing activists.

In 1933, Konoe became president of the upper house, a post his father had held thirty years earlier. In 1934, Konoe went to the United States to attend the high school graduation ceremony of his son but also to have discussions with American politicians, and he noticed the American antipathy toward and distrust of the Japanese. Later in 1936, Japan refused to renew the naval disarmament treaties and walked out of negotiations, further deteriorating Japan's international relations. Konoe continued to argue that the distribution of territories and resources among nations was unfair and a threat to peace, and that America and Britain showed no willingness to recognize and remedy this.

More right-wing assassinations took place in 1936, and the Imperial advisor felt that only Konoe as prime minister could control the military and right-wing elements. Konoe was asked to form a cabinet, but he refused on grounds of poor health. His refusal made him even more conspicuous and raised expectations for him. In May 1937, the cabinet resigned, and this time the Emperor commanded Konoe to form a cabinet. Konoe was 45 and well liked by the public. He was noble and elegant, known to have a superior intellect, and not at all arrogant. The Japanese believed that they were a superior ethnic group and ordained to fulfill a sublime mission, and they looked to Konoe to guide the nation through the turbulent times. The military also welcomed his appointment because they hoped to manipulate him.

The first major international issue that Konoe's cabinet had to contend with was the war in China. One month after the cabinet was formed, Chinese and Japanese troops exchanged fire in the suburbs of Peking. The Army Minister wanted to dispatch more troops to the region. Konoe was afraid of the international repercussions, but eventually he yielded. Konoe tried to establish direct diplomatic contact with Chiang Kai-shek, head of the Nationalist Chinese, and even considered going himself. However, the diplomat he chose to go on the mission was arrested by the Japanese police before he could leave Japan.

The murder of Japanese soldiers in Shanghai led the cabinet to authorize troops to be sent there. The escalation of the war discouraged Konoe. He became dejected and uncertain. Friends encouraged him to finish the task and to be confident in public. He considered dissolving the cabinet but decided to remain to try to restrain the military. As the war continued to take a direction independent of his wishes, his thoughts of resigning became more frequent. Konoe finally resigned in January, 1939, fully aware that his cabinet had been controlled by the military throughout its eighteen months. But Konoe was asked again to form a government in July 1940.

Konoe made great efforts to negotiate with the United States. Contacts were made, and Konoe was eager to meet personally with President Roosevelt. However, the Americans wanted some signs that an agreement could be reached before agreeing to a meeting. Since there was no indication that this could be achieved, the meeting never occurred. The German attack on the Soviet Union in 1941 appalled the Japanese, since it ended hopes of a rapprochement with the Russians.

After the Japanese moved troops to French Indochina in July, 1941, President Roosevelt ordered an embargo on oil exports to Japan and a freeze of all Japanese assets in the United States. Konoe and the military were shocked by this response. The Navy wanted to declare war on the United States immediately, but Konoe was not confident that they could win. He wanted the Navy to restrain the Army's military desires. Konoe tried to prevent a definite decision about the date when hostilities would begin. When the military decided upon October 15, Konoe considered resigning for he did not accept the necessity of hostilities. He was talked out of resigning, and he tried to restrain the military one last time. He failed, and on October 15 he resigned.

On December 8, after the attack on Pearl Harbor, Konoe was shocked, angry, and despondent. Despite the initial victories and the euphoria in Japan, he remained despondent for he was convinced that Japan would eventually lose the war. For the remainder of the war, he remained politically inactive. He was ridiculed and accused of cowardice. He considered renouncing his title and retiring from public life to live in seclusion. However, in 1944, as Japan's impending defeat became obvious, he met with other senior politicians to discuss what could be done. They were concerned about the rise of communism in Japan and the possibility that the communists would use the chaos of defeat to seize power. Konoe tried to get the Emperor to replace Tojo, the prime minister during the war, and to surrender, but he was unsuccessful.

After the surrender of Japan on August 15, 1945, Konoe was blamed by many Japanese for instigating the China War and for facilitating the Pacific War. However, Konoe met with General MacArthur to discuss the situation in Japan and stressed the dangers from left-wing elements. Konoe had at first worried that he might be designated a war criminal, but his meetings with MacArthur reassured him. Konoe got involved with revising the Japanese constitution, but MacArthur's headquarters soon announced that they did not want Konoe to be involved. The New York Times attacked Konoe, and Japanese newspapers took up the attack. On November 9, Konoe was summoned for interrogation on a gunboat (rather than on land as others had been interviewed). He was addressed as Mr. Konoe, and he realized that the Americans saw him as responsible for initiating the China War and planning the war against the United States.

Despite his anxieties, Konoe continued to work on the constitutional revision, and his committee submitted an outline to the Emperor on November 22. At that time he also requested that he be allowed to relinquish his peerage. On November 27, Konoe retired to his country villa and dictated a memoir to a newspaper reporter.

The American command issued lists of war criminals periodically. Eleven people were designated on November 19, and fifty three more on December 2, including an Imperial Prince. Konoe commented that he did not understand why the Prince had not committed suicide. The list of December 6 contained Konoe's name. Colleagues urged Konoe to defend himself and to try to vindicate the Emperor so that the Emperor would not be charged also. Konoe saw the trials as politically motivated and felt that he was powerless to effect any change in the American plans. He said that he could not bear the humiliation of standing in court as a suspected war criminal. He told a newspaper reporter that, before the war, he was ridiculed for being indecisive, during the war rebuked as an escapist peace-seeker, and after the war accused of being a war criminal.

On the day Konoe's arrest order was issued, his brother from whom he had been estranged arrived by ship from Germany where he had spent the war years. They met and repaired their relationship. Konoe was to appear at Sugamo Prison on December 16. Relatives tried to delay his appearance on grounds of ill-health, but any delay was forbidden.

On the evening of December 14, after the last of his friends had departed, Konoe remained with his family and close associates. At 11 o'clock Konoe talked with his second son until 2 a.m. Four hours later, Konoe was found dead in his bed from potassium cyanide poisoning.

7. WILLARD HERSHBERGER:

THE ONLY BASEBALL PLAYER TO KILL

HIMSELF DURING THE SEASON

13,123 players and managers in the baseball major leagues have been identified for the period 1871 to 1987 and, of these, 6,374 have been verified to have died, with 578 more dead but unverified. Of those deceased, 64 are known to be suicides and, of these, only one is known to have committed suicide during the baseball season, Willard Hershberger. Hershberger was the backup catcher for the Cincinnati Reds, and he killed himself at the Copley Plaza Hotel in Boston on August 3, 1940.

Hershberger was small and light for a catcher — 5′ 10″ and 160 pounds. His ancestry was Scots, Irish and German, and he was born on May 28, 1911, in California. He had brown eyes and dark hair and was right-handed. He never married. His hobbies were ranching, hunting, and amateur radio work.

He was not the first-string catcher and usually caught only in the second game of double-headers or pinch-hit. He had traveled around the minor leagues (Binghamton, El Paso, Erie, Hollywood, Newark, Oakland and Springfield), but he had been voted the International League catcher in 1937. In 1938 he batted .276 for the Reds and .345 the following year when they won the pennant.

In July 1940, the Reds' catcher sprained an ankle, and Hershberger took over. He was batting .362. The Reds began a road trip on July 23, seven games in front of the second-place team. They won the first four games, and Hershberger hit well, but he then went three for twenty in the next five games he caught. The temperature on the East Coast was in the 90s and that was thought to be responsible for Hershberger's decline. On July 27 the Reds lost to the Phillies in 100° weather, and the next day they played a double-header in 99° weather. Hershberger was clearly suffering from dehydration.

Next at New York, in the third game of the series, the Reds were one strike from the victory but lost. Hershberger blamed himself for the loss — he thought he had called the wrong pitches. At Boston, Hershberger went hitless in his first game, and he seemed catatonic behind the plate. His manager talked to Hershberger back at the hotel, and Hershberger sobbed and talked of ending his life. He confessed that he had attempted suicide in the past but failed. He also revealed that his father had committed suicide. He felt responsible for the recent losses and for letting the team down. However, at the time of his suicide, the Reds had a six game lead in the National League and Hershberger was hitting a respectable .309.

The next day, Saturday, the Reds were playing a double-header with the Boston Bees. Hershberger did not report to the ballpark, and his manager was alarmed. The traveling secretary called the hotel, and Hershberger answered and said he felt ill. He promised to come down. but he still had not arrived after the first game. The manager then dispatched a friend of Hershberger's to the hotel who found Hershberger in the bathroom. He had covered the floor with towels and slashed his throat with his roommate's safety razor while leaning over the bathtub.

After Hershberger's suicide, his teammates recalled that he had been depressed throughout the season. He had always suffered from insomnia, and now he frequently complained of headaches. He had bought an insurance policy before leaving for the road trip and had asked a friend to make sure his mother got his car and a bond should anything happen to him. He had referred to suicide several times during the season and twice the day before he died.

Hershberger's father killed himself November 21, 1929. He had been depressed for several weeks, with financial worries and a demotion at work. He shot himself in the chest in the bathroom of his house at 2.30 am with a shotgun, leaving a bloody mess for his family to find. Hershberger did his best to be tidier in his death than his father had been.

8. ELVIS PRESLEY:

THE KING OF ROCK AND ROLL

When Albert Goldman wrote his biography of Elvis Presley in 1981, he concluded that Elvis's death was caused by an accidental overdose of drugs. In 1990, Goldman revised his view and decided that Elvis's death was, in fact, a suicide.

Elvis was born in East Tupelo in the northeast corner of Mississippi. His father's family came from Britain in the 1740s but never rose to much — Elvis's father, Vernon, was illiterate. His mother's family, the Smiths, originated in the Carolinas. In the early days, a couple of first cousins married, and their offspring had a high incidence of addiction, emotional disorders and early death. Elvis had three uncles on his mother's side. One was born deaf, and one died early (as did Elvis's mother). Two were heavy drinkers and violent when drunk. One of Elvis's cousins committed suicide with arsenic.

Gladys Smith met Vernon Presley when she was twenty and he was sixteen. They fell in love and married on June 17, 1933. Gladys was a hard worker and an ebullient extravert. Vernon was a shirker and a dullard. At first they lived with Vernon's parents in East Tupelo, but they eventually moved to a two-room cabin built by Vernon on a lot owned by his father.

Gladys was soon pregnant, and she was convinced she had twins. On the morning of January 8, 1935, Gladys delivered a stillborn son and then Elvis. Gladys claimed that they were identical twins, but there is no evidence for this. Gladys was told she could not bear children again, and she grieved deeply for her lost son. Gladys talked about him constantly, often taking Elvis to the cemetery. Gladys built up a myth around this twin, telling Elvis that the dead twin's personality was transferred to him. When Elvis was four or five, he began to hear this dead twin talk to him.

Two years after Elvis's birth, Gladys's mother died (her father had already died), and Gladys, once cheerful, now became depressed. Then in 1937, Vernon Presley was arrested for forging a check and sentenced to three years in the state penitentiary. He was discharged in January 1941. He then spent the war years working in a defense plant in Memphis, coming home only on weekends.

Elvis was raised, therefore, alone with his mother from the age of three to about eleven and became a classic mama's boy. Gladys worshipped him, spoilt him, but also severely restricted him out of fear for his safety. He was reared to be a recluse. They slept in the same bed. Elvis was physically affectionate with his mother till her death, and they had a set of affectionate terms and baby language for each other. Elvis was accustomed to sharing all of his thoughts with Gladys and, in later life, was very dependent on her opinion.

Though the family belonged to the Assembly of God which forbad movies, dancing, alcohol and tobacco, Elvis heard music on the radio, and he won a prize for singing at the annual Mississippi-Alabama Fair and Dairy Show when he was eleven.

In 1948, the family moved to Memphis to look for work. Elvis majored in shop at high school, obtained mediocre grades, and was socially invisible. Gladys did not permit Elvis to play out of her sight until he was fifteen! However, Elvis managed to acquire a steady girl friend who tried, unsuccessfully, to teach Elvis to dance the two-step. Elvis would often play the guitar and sing outside the house for neighbors, but his shyness made him wait until it was dark. After his second girl friend broke up with him, he never dated again in high school.

In 1951, he shocked the school by appearing with a

classic Duck's Ass hair style inspired by Tony Curtis, and he began to wear colorful clothes. This was the beginning of the emergence of the bad-assed Elvis, which he developed within a few years into a tough punk image. (At the same time, he was in ROTC, trying for the football team and planning to become a state police officer or a lay priest.) Finally in his senior year, he was persuaded to sing at the school, and the kids were amazed at how well he performed.

After high school he got a job driving a truck and tried singing in the various clubs around Memphis. He went to a local studio just to see how he sounded and recorded two songs by the Ink Spots. The recording engineer remembered a colleague wishing he could find a white who could sing like a black, and he thought Elvis would do. So in July 1954, Elvis went back to the studio — singing in a country style with a rhythm and blues beat. This first record rose to number three on Memphis's country and western charts two weeks after release. After singing in public, his musicians told him that the way he shook his leg had the audience screaming. Elvis's style began to take shape.

There quickly followed an appearance at the Grand Ole Opry where he flopped and then on Louisiana Hayride where he was a success. He was given a one year contract, and Elvis worked every small town in the region. These shows and his records on radio made him sell-known in the south. In November 1954, Elvis quit his job as a truck driver and got a personal manager, Bob Neal, who ran shows in school houses and on radio. Elvis bought his first Cadillac, pink and black, and a house for his family. Vernon retired (at the age of thirty-eight) and never worked again.

Colonel Tom Parker, though no Colonel, met Elvis in 1955. Parker managed one performer at a time and had recently managed Eddie Arnold for nine years. He was raised on the circus and fair ground circuits and approached managing performers in the same style. He saw great potential in Elvis and had managed to sign on as his personal manager by August 1955.

Parker's influence on Elvis was great and not altogether good. He did help Elvis become a star. However, on the negative side, because his own fear of investments and the government, he avoided investing Elvis's money or setting up tax shelters with the result that Elvis did not build up a fortune, paid enormous sums to the Internal Revenue Service and was severely short of money in his later years.

Parker was also not interested in developing Elvis's talents. Rather he wanted to exploit what Elvis could do. So Parker signed him up (at relatively low pay) to do an interminable series of poor movies. Elvis himself at first had hopes of becoming a good movie actor, but the films that Parker had him make destroyed those desires. After the movie career was over, he had Elvis give an endless round of stage performances (again at less than Elvis could have earned).

But, back in 1956, Elvis recorded his first records for RCA and soon was at the top of the charts. By the end of the year he had been acclaimed as the King of Rock and Roll. He stopped touring in 1957 to concentrate on movies. Only in the 1970s when his movies were no longer marketable did he resume touring.

Despite his considerable talent, Elvis's lack of education and musical skills led him to become dependent on others. Elvis could not write his own material, and he was not focussed enough to know what he ought to have performed. He let his manager and the record company feed him a steady stream of songs which they thought would be successful, songs which after his spell in the army led him away from rhythm and blues towards crooning.

Similarly in his movies, he was clear about his goal of becoming a good screen actor (James Dean was his idol), but he was not focussed enough to reject shoddy scripts. He accepted them, while recognizing that they were shoddy, completing twenty nine movies in all.

The result was that, although audiences still energized him, his work depressed him. For example, in 1964, Parker decreed that Elvis would record only the movie soundtrack albums. Elvis thought that these songs were terrible and often exploded in anger and frustration in the studios. But his dejection led him to relinquish even more control over the recording sessions. Elvis always gave in to the crass commercialism of his handlers, becoming more bitter, cynical and estranged all the while.

In 1968, the fortunes of Elvis continued their decline, especially in the face of the Beatles, the British Invasion and psychedelic music. Parker signed Elvis to perform in a special on television which happened to be directed and arranged by some very talented people. Elvis, now thirty-three, looked great. In front of a live audience for the first time since he was twenty-two in the late 1950s, Elvis was terrified, but the music was good. Elvis began a new stage in his career, recording much better songs with vastly improved musicians and appearing on stage mostly in Las Vegas. But soon, the exploitation turned into a treadmill — seven years of four week appearances every February and August at the International Hotel in Las Vegas.

Early on, Gladys feared that Elvis's nightmares and sleepwalking might get him into trouble. So she encouraged him to take along friends as guardians. At first, his two cousins accompanied him, but soon the entourage grew. These aides would, for very meager wages, and occasional large presents, orchestrate Elvis's life for him, from procuring girls to guarding his life from potential death threats. They were with him constantly and were his friends, though never equals. They were at his mercy, and toward the end of his life

Elvis fired or was left by almost all of those who had accompanied him for the twenty or so years of his stardom. Elvis replaced them with his kid step-brothers and hired bodyguards. In many ways, Elvis was a recluse, but he was a recluse in the midst of these men. Their marriages broke up because of the demands Elvis made on them, and one even attempted suicide when his wife left him.

After his army service, Elvis lost a great deal of self-confidence. From being confident and strong, he became delicate and vulnerable. Instead of partying with his peers, he locked himself up in Graceland and other venues with his aides. Instead of courting film stars, he had anonymous groupies trooped through his bedroom.

Soon, Elvis developed a stable sexual pattern. He liked virgins, particularly teenagers. He liked to chat for hours, wrestle, have pillow fights, tickle and sleep (literally) with them. But he did not like to have sex with them. The majority of the girls stayed virgins. From being sexually excited by pubic hairs peeking through the white panties of small kittenish girls, he moved to enjoying them interacting sexually. Eventually he made home videos of these scenes. (He also liked to watch his aides have sex with women.) He would masturbate while watching the women, and occasionally he would be able to quickly have sexual intercourse with one of them once stimulated. He abhorred married women and those who had given birth.

On the other hand, he did like to have a steady girl friend, and he managed to have a succession of such women who pandered to his needs. The first few were eventually replaced by a fourteen year-old whom he met in August 1959 when serving in the army in Germany, Priscilla, whom he promised to marry if her parents would let her go to live with him (which she did in May 1962), and whom he was forced into marrying (in May 1967). As soon as she gave birth to a daughter in February 1968, she became sexually unexciting to him, and she was replaced by a new series of girl friends. Elvis's pattern with women moved from romantic courtship, to play in which the woman was supposed to take more initiative, ending with Elvis as the baby and the woman as the adoring caretaking mother.

Early in his career, Elvis developed into a spendthrift. He would rent a roller skating rink at midnight for a party and movie theaters for his own private showings of movies; or have the state police shut down a stretch of Highway 51 for motor bike racing.

By the age of forty, Elvis had earned a hundred million dollars and was broke. Spending sprees such as buying fourteen Cadillacs one night in Memphis (and giving one away to a black woman who was passing by), setting up friends in new houses, buying four aircraft, giving away jewelry during his performances, quickly ate up his money. One night in 1975, in Graceland, Elvis and his aides remembered the peanut butter and jelly sandwiches they had once in Denver. They flew down to get them, picked them up at the airport and flew back to Graceland. Sixteen thousand dollars for sandwiches. To pay for all of this, Elvis was forced to work. In 1974, he played 152 shows, two-thirds of which were one night stands.

Prior to the 1960s, Elvis took amphetamines, but not to excess. After his army service he began to consume a whole range of drugs, including stimulants, narcotics and hypnotics. Elvis always had trouble sleeping, so it was natural to him to start taking downers. He (and his aides) took Dexamil, Quaaludes, Percodan, Demerol, Seconal, Tuinal, Valium, Nembutal and Placidyl. During the years in which he made three depressing movies a year in Hollywood, Elvis's consumption of drugs increased. Eventually he added Dilaudid. In the last two and a half years of his life, Elvis received 19,000 doses of drugs from one physician alone, and he used the services of many physicians.

Elvis never saw himself as a drug addict. For Elvis, "addicts" used heroin and injected it into their veins. He did not do this. (He did have others skin-pop drugs into him on occasions.) Indeed, he presented himself as a friend of law enforcement, opposed to hippies and drug abusers, collecting police badges and trying to get the President and the FBI to use him to fight drug abuse.

Soon Elvis's depressions grew serious. In the Spring of 1964, Elvis locked himself in the bedroom at Graceland and refused to speak with anyone. This first serious depression was broken by the arrival of a hairdresser (Larry Geller) who was into spiritualism and got Elvis interested in the occult. In 1967, Elvis's manager managed to get Elvis married to Priscilla and rid of Larry Geller at the same time. Elvis now began to overeat when depressed, a diet of especially fattening proportions, including corn pone, mashed potatoes, and cheeseburgers. At times his weight rose to over 255 pounds.

Elvis feared growing old. Happiness was possible only in youth, he believed. He watched the mirrors constantly for signs of aging. His hair turned grey, but it was of course dyed. He had a face-lift, and he hid his 'chicken' neck with high collars.

The first threats on his life led Elvis to buy guns for himself and for his aides. After the Sharon Tate murders in 1969, Elvis bought over 250 guns, armed his aides, and kept a gun with him at all times. And in August 1970 there was indeed a serious threat on Elvis's life made during a Las Vegas appearance.

Soon after the birth of her daughter, Priscilla fell in love with a karate performer, Mike Stone. They concealed their affair for over three years which was easy since Elvis no longer had any sexual involvement with Priscilla and was absent most of the time. She told

Elvis in February 1972 and left him. Elvis fell into a deep depression, and his drug consumption soared. His aides tried to entice him with new women to replace Priscilla, but he called Priscilla every night and threatened to have her lover killed, threats he continued to make for the next year and a half. His anger eventually dissipated somewhat when he met Linda Thompson, Miss Tennessee of 1972, a virgin, and willing to adapt to Elvis's life style for the next four years. He was even faithful for a year, and Linda accepted his infidelities after that. He regressed back to infancy with Linda. She called him Baby Buntin while he called her Mommy. She would feed him by hand, read to him while he lay in bed in diapers, and administer his drugs. During this period he finally became a hopelessly addicted junkie and a bloated dysfunctional person. The only activities which could reverse this state were his public performances which inspired him to cut down on the drugs and lose weight.

In 1973, Priscilla went to court to change the ridiculously low settlement she had obtained. Elvis now began to behave even more crazily than ever. His behavior became more erratic, even during his performances. After his August shows in Las Vegas, he and a teenage fan were found comatose after an overdose of a narcotic cough syrup.

All of Elvis's intimates agree that the fatal decline which ended with his death began during the break up with Priscilla when his wife rejected him for another man. In 1976, some of his aides whom he had fired negotiated to write a book about Elvis, and Linda finally called it quits. Although Elvis found a replacement (Ginger Alden), she refused to move in with him or travel with him on his tours. The book (Elvis — What Happened) appeared in July 1977, detailing his reckless drug abuse. Elvis found out about the book just before he was to begin his tour during which he would have to

43

face the public after the revelations of his drug abuse and sexual habits. There was a good chance that the audience and press would be quite negative. He was also close to bankruptcy.

On August 15, 1977, Elvis was about to leave for a twelve-day concert tour. He awoke at four in the afternoon and drank coffee (he was fasting). He planned to watch movies at midnight, but no projectionist could be found. He went for a dental appointment at ten in the evening, and at two-thirty on the morning called his doctor's nurse for some Dilaudid. He sat up talking with Ginger, planning their wedding, and at four in the morning called up an aide to play racquetball. At six thirty he took more drugs and again at eight. Fifteen minutes later he called his doctor's nurse for more pills which were sent over. Ginger went to sleep and woke up at two in the afternoon. She found Elvis dead in the bathroom. The autopsy identified eleven drugs in his body, including anti-depressants.

In retrospect, there were many instances of suicidal communications by Elvis in the days prior to his death. After watching an old television show of his, Elvis said, "I may not look good now, but I'll look good in my coffin." After seeing Priscilla, a step-brother told Elvis, "You'll see her again," but Elvis replied, "We'll see." Elvis was observed praying, "God, help me! I can't go on." When his step-brother left two days before Elvis died, Elvis told him that they would never meet again. Finally, there is evidence of a history of suicide attempts — an attempt with barbiturates in 1967 after an argument with Priscilla, seriously enough to lose consciousness.

There are many interesting features of Elvis's life, but what seems most important is Elvis's arrested development. His early dependence on his mother, made stronger by the death of his twin and the absences of his father, created an immaturity that Elvis never overcame. His wealth and power enabled him to perpetuate this dependency on women, so that he could recreate an infantile dependency in his relationships with young women. Toward the end of his life he became less able to do this. Priscilla left him, followed four years later by Linda. Ginger refused to play the role of mother.

As his life drew toward its close, there were other stresses too – a chronic life of dissatisfaction with his career – forced to star in bad movies, sing bad songs, and tour unendingly because he lacked the assertiveness and goal-directedness (and perhaps talent) to give his artistic career the direction it needed. His impulsive overspending was leading him toward bankruptcy, and his hostility toward his aides led to their public disclosure of his drug and sexual habits. He would no longer be able to maintain the public image he once had enjoyed.

Finally, there were deep depressions which the chronic drug abuse, spending sprees and adulation of teenage fans had masked. The depressions and the drug abuse worsened as women and aides deserted him (or were dismissed). Elvis was a high risk candidate for suicide at the time of death, and so perhaps Goldman was correct in his reassessment of Elvis's death.

9. SERGEI ESENIN:

ISADORA DUNCAN'S RUSSIAN

HUSBAND

Sergei Esenin was born on October 3, 1895, the son of a peasant in Konstantinovo in the province of Ryazan in Central Russia. He was raised by his maternal grandparents since his parents lived apart for most of his childhood. His father lived in Moscow, and his mother gave birth to another child which his father refused to acknowledge. Sergei felt as if he were an orphan.

He attended the local primary school from the ages of nine to fourteen and then moved to a church boarding school. He was able, mischievous and a fighter. Sergei did not enjoy school and declined to go to the Moscow Teacher's Institute. Instead, arriving in Moscow in July 1812, he worked in a butcher's shop, at a bookshop, and in a printing works, and sometimes attended lectures in the evening. In the big city, he gave up vegetarianism and began to smoke and drink.

He had begun to write poems while at school, and he continued to do so in Moscow. He joined a literary society where he recited his poems and soon he was able to get his poems published. He joined up with other peasant poets, and they dressed in peasant costumes and gave recitations at fashionable salons. Although there was criticism of his work, his popularity grew, and he became arrogant and ambitious.

He was called into military service in 1916 but avoided onerous duties. He may even have recited his verse to the Empress. After the revolution in 1917, Sergei's poems were criticized by the Marxists. Sergei, who had been living near St. Petersburg since 1915, moved back to Moscow in 1918 and joined up with fellow poets to form a group called the Imaginists. The Imaginists rejected the idea that poems should have content, and they liked eccentric and coarse imagery. They set up a publishing firm and bookshops and read their poems in bohemian restaurants, including a cafe they ran themselves.

The group gained notoriety and success. Sergei gave up his peasant costumes and now dressed as a dandy. He cultivated the image of a hooligan, behaving irresponsibly for publicity, such as writing obscene verses on convent walls. He lived with his friends when he was not traveling around Russia, and this period was remarkably productive and reasonably happy for Sergei. However, there were already premonitions of boredom and depression. He began to drink excessively and, when he was drunk, became bitter, arrogant, intolerant, self-pitying and hypersensitive.

Sergei had first fallen in love with a village girl when he was fifteen. In Moscow, he fell in love with a woman, Anna, with whom he lived, and they had son in 1915. Nevertheless, he abandoned them to go to St. Petersburg later that year. In 1917, he married a secretary, Zinaida, but they parted within two years and divorced in 1921. Zinaida had two children, but Sergei believed that the second was not his. Most of Sergei's friends believed that Sergei loved Zinaida more than any other woman in his life. Many of Sergei's male friends were infatuated with him, and some biographers have speculated that Sergei was a latent homosexual.

The American dancer, Isadora Duncan, decided to visit Russia in 1921. She was forty-four and Sergei was almost twenty-six when they met. They seemed to be attracted to each other immediately, and Sergei moved into Isadora's apartment in Moscow. Isadora was instantly captivated by Sergei and saw him as the lover for her autumn years. Isadora's two children had drowned earlier, and Sergei may have reminded Isadora of her son. Sergei was captivated by Isadora's fame and the life she could promise him. However he was tyrannical toward Isadora from the first, beating her and insulting her.

Isadora's life was one of excess too. Although Sergei had drank a lot before meeting Isadora, the wild parties night after night at Isadora's apartment soon increased Sergei's intake until he was truly an alcoholic. In 1920 and 1921, Sergei maintained his life with the poets and his life with Isadora, but he grew increasingly ill and depressed. He described himself as tired, wretched and corrupt. In time Isadora won out over the poets. Once Sergei's divorce from Zinaida was granted in 1921, Isadora and he planned a trip abroad where she would dance and he would recite his poetry. Sergei and Isadora were married on May 2, 1922, and they left by plane for Germany on May 10.

Their travels took them to first to Germany where there was a large Russian émigré group, then Belgium, France, Italy, America, and back to France. Isadora danced, and Sergei recited and arranged for the translation and publication of his poems. But Isadora received more attention, especially since Sergei could speak only Russian. (In fact, Isadora spoke hardly any Russian and had great difficulty communicating with Sergei.) The course of their travels involved expensive hotels, excessive drinking, and incessant quarrels. They did very little sight-seeing, and Sergei hated every place they visited.

As the trip progressed, Sergei's behavior grew increasingly uncontrolled, and he began to break apart the furniture in the hotels they stayed in until many hotels refused to let them stay. Sergei, depressed, bored and now homesick, continued to drink heavily. He first threatened suicide in Berlin and continued to talk of it from time to time. He also ran away from Isadora for days at a time. Sergei tried on several occasions to give up drinking because of his poor health, but he found life without alcohol unbearable.

Back in France in February 1923, Sergei's feelings of inferiority as a Russian peasant in the civilized world and as being viewed simply as Isadora's lover, combined with his drunkenness, led to more fights with Isadora and great destruction in the hotels. Within a week, Sergei had fled to Berlin leaving Isadora in France.

Isadora traveled to Berlin in March to see Sergei and, despite more fights and expulsions from hotels, they returned to Paris together in April. Sergei's behavior led to his arrest, but Isadora managed to get him transferred to a private clinic. Finally, in July they left for Moscow. Soon after their arrival in Moscow, Isadora left for a dance tour in the Caucasus. Sergei immediately moved out of Isadora's apartment and went to live with a former colleague. He soon became attached to a nurse, Galina Benislavskaya, and in September moved in with her. Sergei telegraphed Isadora that he was in love with another and had married her!

When Isadora returned to Moscow, Sergei hid from her. They eventually did meet on a couple of occasions, but the relationship was never resumed. Isadora eventually left Russia without him in September 1924.

Meanwhile, Sergei fell in love with an actress, but their relationship soon petered out. He became estranged from his Imaginist poet friends. He had spells in hospitals, a possible suicide attempt, and eventually left for the Caucasus in September 1924 for a six month rest. He returned to Moscow in March 1925 where he fell in love with Sofia Tolstaya, a granddaughter of Tolstoy. He continued to wander restlessly about Russia, but in June he decided to marry Sofia, and he left Galina to live with Sofia. They married in September even though he had never obtained a divorce from Isadora. He still wrote prolifically, often on the theme of death. In December, he entered a psychiatric clinic with alcoholic hallucinations and delirium tremens. He left after a month against the doctor's advice.

He spent the next few days in Moscow, drinking, gathering his belongings and saying goodbye to friends. He left Moscow for Leningrad, arriving there on December 24. He spent the next two days quietly, visiting a friend on December 25th. In the early hours of December 27th, he wrote a brief poem in his blood. He was found hanging from a pipe in his room on the morning of December 28th, 1925.

Sergei's life was beginning to show signs of self-destructive decline before he met Isadora Duncan. But his involvement with her hastened the end. With her, his drinking and uncontrollable behavior increased, and his self-esteem suffered, especially on the trip abroad where he was clearly not held in as great esteem as his middle-aged wife. However, back in Russia, though he managed to write, he failed to find satisfying relationships, and he continued to drink. His depression and despair grew and, after his last attempt to give up drinking, he decided to kill himself. What is surprising is the speed of his decline — fame by the age of twenty and alcoholism and death by the age of thirty. Perhaps he would have been dead by then even without Isadora?

10. PAUL KAMMERER:

ACCUSED OF SCIENTIFIC FRAUD

Paul Kammerer went for a walk on September 23, 1926, on an Austrian mountain path. He sat down against a rock and shot himself in the head. His suicide note bequeathed his body to a university for dissection and said, in part, "Perhaps my worthy academic colleagues will discover in my brain a trace of the qualities they found absent from the manifestations of my mental activities while I was alive."

Paul had been accused of fraud in his scientific work, and his suicide seems to have been motivated in part by the stress of these accusations and by anger at those who had accused him. His suicide had the result, however, of convincing most of those involved that he must have been guilty of the fraud.

The Darwinians believed that evolution proceeded through genetic mutations (and of course your genes are fixed at the moment of your conception), while the Lamarckians believed that characteristics that you acquire during your life can be passed on to your offspring. According to Darwinians, if you are very intelligent, it is because your genes predispose you to be intelligent. Your offspring will probably be very intelligent too because they inherit your genes. The Lamarckians believe that, whatever your genes, if you develop your intelligent abilities during your life prior to having children, your children may be high in intelligence because they inherit this acquired intelligence from you. Lamarckians could not propose any mechanism to account for the transmission of the acquired characteristics through the fertilization of eggs by the sperm, and so it was viewed as a superstition rather than a theory.

Of course, the power struggles have an extra layer of complexity, since the free world adopted the Darwinian idea while the Communists, newly in power in Russia, adopted the Lamarckian idea. (When he killed himself, Paul was packed, ready to go to Russia to pursue his research there.) And today, Christians in parts of the United States try to suppress Darwin's ideas in school textbooks because it conflicts with their ideas of the appearance of humans on earth, ideas based on the Bible. Darwin's ideas have clearly aroused intense emotions and conflicts between believers and nonbelievers.

Paul was born on August 17, 1880, of Saxon ancestors who now lived in Austria. His family was prosperous, for his father, Karl, was the founder and co-proprietor of a factory for making optical instruments. After twenty years of marriage, Karl divorced his wife and married a Hungarian widow, Sophie. (It was her third marriage, and she had two sons from previous marriages, while Karl had one.) Paul was born with three step-brothers, aged eighteen to twenty, who adored him.

In this setting, Paul developed into a bright child. His childhood seems uneventful, and he began by studying music at the Vienna Academy. He composed songs that were performed in Vienna, and he counted among his friends Bruno Walter, later a famous conductor, and Gustav Mahler, the composer. Paul then switched to reading zoology at the University, and some biologists held his early interest in music against Paul. They saw him as a dilettante.

Paul had grown up with an interest in and an affinity for animals. His early articles were on reptiles and amphibians and published in naturalist journals. These articles were read by the eminent biologist Hans Przibram who was founding an Institute for Experimental Biology, which was a new branch of research, a break from the theoretical and descriptive zoology currently in vogue.

Paul began by organizing the aquaria and terraria and proved to be very successful in keeping the animals alive in these unnatural conditions. This point is of importance to the story because others could not replicate Paul's experiments (to see if they would get the same results as he claimed) because none of them could keep the animals alive in the laboratory.

In 1909, Paul received a scientific prize for his research on salamanders. He also conducted research on the sea-squirt, and later on the midwife toad, and it was this latter research that became the battle ground. The research in question was published between 1906 and 1919 in three major papers.

Paul also gave popular lectures on biology in general, and on his research in particular, which were very popular. These too were frowned upon by leading academics because it an unwritten rule that serious scientists do not seek popular fame.

The battle over Paul's research was fought in England and published mainly in the scientific journal Nature. The major accuser was William Bateson. Interestingly, Bateson had started by believing in the Lamarckian hypothesis. But after a fruitless expedition to Central Asia to search for confirmation, he switched to believing Darwinism. (Bateson named his son after the Russian geneticist Gregor Mendel, whose work had contributed an important element to Darwinian theory.)

Bateson visited Vienna in 1910. He already thought that Paul's work was fraudulent, and his belief was confirmed when Paul could not produce specimens of the midwife toad to show the acquired characteristics. These characteristics, pads on the forearms of the toad, appear only in the mating season, and Bateson was not in Vienna during the toads' mating season.

The problem of verifying Paul's work was made complicated by the First World War, which led to the destruction of many of the specimens in the Institute.

Most of the animals died during this period. Paul himself was excused from military service because of a heart condition, but was assigned to military duties (censoring the letters from Italian prisoners) and so could not continue his research. Following the war, the inflation in Austria led to the ruin of many, including Przibram and Kammerer. The Biological Institute was taken over by the Austrian Academy of Science.

All that remained to show sceptics were some slides and specimens preserved in jars. In 1920, the Institute sent Bateson some slides of the pads on the midwife toad, but he regarded them too as frauds, probably cut from a different species of toad. Once Bateson had made up his mind, nothing would change it.

In 1923 Paul was invited to visit England to lecture on his research. He did so and brought with him a preserved specimen of the midwife toad showing the pads. Interestingly, Bateson did not attend the first lecture, but did attend the second. At the second lecture he did not examine the specimen. Bateson, firmly believing that Kammerer had faked his research, declined to examine the evidence.

However, after Paul had returned to Vienna, Bateson wrote requesting that the specimen be sent to him for examination! The Institute refused, for it was the sole remaining specimen and Bateson had declined to view it four months earlier. Bateson saw this refusal as proof of the fraud.

Paul resigned from his post at the Institute in order to support his family by journalism and lecturing. He went twice to the United States for lecture tours (in the Fall of 1923 and the Spring of 1924). One unfortunate consequence of his lectures in England and the United States was that the newspapers wrote up his ideas sensationally. Headlines read Race Of Supermen in London and Scientist Tells Of Success Where Darwin Met Failure in New York. This publicity further alienated scholars in the field. Paul also gave lecture tours in the Soviet Union which led to his being invited to assume the position of Professor of Genetics at Pavlov's Experimental Institute in Moscow.

The final episode occurred in 1926 when G. Noble from the American Museum of Natural History in New York City, went to Vienna, cut the specimen of the midwife toad and found that the markings were due to injections of ink. He published the finding in Nature, together with a report by Przibram confirming Noble's findings. Paul shot himself six weeks later.

Paul's personal life added to his stress. Paul joined the Biological Institute in 1903 at the age of twenty-three. He got his doctorate in 1904 and became a lecturer at the University in 1906. In 1905 he met the young Baroness Felicitas Maria Theodore von Wiedersperg, fell in love at once, and after the customary year-long engagement was married in 1906. The Wiederspergs shared Paul's interest in music and animals, and so he got on well with his in-laws. Paul had a daughter in 1907, and he named her Lacerta after a genus of lizards.

Paul seems to have been a philanderer. After Gustav Mahler's death in 1911, his widow Alma worked as Paul's laboratory assistant and had an affair with Paul. Soon after this affair, Paul fell in love with a painter, Anna Walt. Felicitas agreed to a divorce on grounds of mutual incompatibility in order to let him marry Anna, but the marriage lasted only a few months. After a row with Anna, Paul swallowed an overdose of sleeping pills but vomited them up. He became depressed, and returned to live with Felicitas. (His marriage to Anna was annulled, and his marriage to Felicitas restored.)

After his return to Vienna from the United States in 1924 he fell in love again. He was attracted to the five Weisenthal sisters and fell in love with most of them before settling on Grete, the oldest. (Paul's daughter thinks that at least two of the romances were platonic.)

Grete was forty and married, and it is not known whether she reciprocated Paul's love. Their liaison was widely talked about in Vienna. However, Grete refused to accompany Paul to Moscow.

By 1926 Paul's world was in ruin. He had been accused of faking his research. He had popular fame, but scholarly scorn. His collection of specimens had been destroyed. He was poor and unable to support his family (though this was true of many Austrians at the time).

Paul in the final years of his life alternated between depression and mania, but continued to work hard. (In addition to writing and lecturing, he wrote a book on biology based on field trips he took to the Dalmatian Isles to study lizards.)

Paul had been offered a position by the Moscow Academy of Sciences as Professor of Genetics and was due to begin his work in Moscow on October 1. He visited the Soviet legation in Vienna on September 20 with instructions for the packing and transportation of his scientific apparatus. On the day he shot himself, his furniture was being packed for removal to Moscow. In a suicide note addressed to the Moscow Academy of Sciences, he denied participating in the forgery but declined their offer because he no longer felt himself to be qualified for the position. (A newspaper report after Paul's death claimed that he planned to stay in Moscow only a short time and that he hoped that his work there would lead to an offer from a German university. The discovery of the forged specimen made such an invitation extremely unlikely.) Perhaps the final straw was that Grete Weisenthal, with whom he was in love, had refused to accompany him to Moscow. His suicide notes reflect the complexity of the motivations for his suicide, for he wrote notes to the Moscow Academy of Sciences, his wife Felicitas and his lover Grete Weisenthal.

11. FREDDIE PRINZE:

YOUNG COMEDIAN

Freddie Prinze, a successful comedian, was only twenty-two when he shot himself. He had performed at the pre-inaugural ball for President Carter only ten days earlier. He was not someone who had been successful and who was now facing a decline. Rather he was a star on the way up. How did he come to kill himself?

Frederick Karl Pruetzel was born on June 22, 1954, in New York City. His mother, Maria, was an immigrant from Puerto Rico and his father, Karl, was Hungarian and an immigrant from Germany. Karl, had been married before and had three children. (Both Karl and his son Freddie were only children of second marriages and unusually close to their mothers.) During his first marriage, Karl was painting his house one day, and his five year old daughter drowned in the swimming pool. He was too late to save her, and he blamed himself for her death. He drank heavily, though the drinking did not affect his work. His second wife, Maria, felt that this experience reinforced his fear of taking responsibility for his son Freddie. Since Karl also worked nights, he spent little time with his son, though Karl and Freddie did things together on weekends and holidays (such as horseback riding). However, Maria more or less raised Freddie by herself. Maria lived near to her family (her sisters even had an apartment in the same building, and her brother and then her father lived with her for a time), and so all of the relatives helped take care of Freddie and showered him with love. Freddie was the only baby in this extended family, and so Freddie was pampered.

Initially, Freddie went to the public schools where he suffered from bullying and extortion. He was fat as a child which may have helped make him a victim. He often cried over the stress of attending the school.

He took four years of piano lessons and then switched to the guitar. Maria bought him a guitar for $150 when he was fourteen, and he worked hard to learn it. Interestingly, the pampering is evident in the circumstances surrounding the purchase of the guitar. His mother bought him it in exchange for him painting the apartment. He painted a little and then persuaded his mother to do the rest. She acquiesced.

Toward the end of his stay at the public school, he became the class clown. He skipped classes, and his academic grades declined. However, he lost his childhood pudginess, and he received school awards for his music and dramatic abilities.

In the Fall of 1970, he was accepted at the High School of the Performing Arts in New York City, and Maria was made anxious by her son becoming independent from her. Freddie persuaded Maria to give him seventy dollars a week so that he could take a taxi to school. He liked being driven in style to the school in front of the students and teachers. To get more money, he took an ushering job at a movie theater.

In the summer of 1971, he performed in musical shows for the Alliance of Latin Art, and he decided to join a rock band at the school. So he persuaded his mother to get him a job at her factory, where he worked hard and earned enough to buy some drums. (He paid half, and his mother paid half.) In the Fall of 1971, he joined the band as drummer.

In his second year, his friends suggested that he develop his comic skills, and so he began performing at the comedy clubs in the city. In the summer of 1972, he decided to quit the Alliance musical shows and the rock band, and to focus on comedy. He went from club to club, moving up in status as a comedian yet, when his act did not go over well with the audience, he would become depressed. Academically, Freddie performed badly, failing English, history, economics and Spanish. He refused to go to summer school, and he dropped out of school in 1973.

In 1973, Freddie changed his name from Pruetzel to Prinze and began to focus on his career as a comic. His talent enabled him to move up to better clubs, and he acquired a manager, David Jonas.

By the end of 1973, Freddie was appearing on television shows (Jack Paar and eventually the Tonight Show). In 1974 he auditioned for and was given a part in Chico And The Man on NBC television. He liked Los Angeles and decided to stay there, but he missed his girl friend who had refused to go with him. He described himself as lonely and depressed. He had developed the habit of using the telephone to keep in touch with people, running up bills of $800 a month. In his diary, he wrote that there was no one there to protect him. He called home nightly.

While in Los Angeles, his producer, Jimmy Komack, found out that Freddie was using cocaine (in addition to valium and quaaludes). He sent him to a physician, Edward Ablon, who continued to prescribe him quaaludes until his suicide.

After Chico And The Man aired, although it was a success, Freddie got anonymous death threats. (Chicanos were upset over the way in which Freddie was depicting one of their ethnic group.) In October, 1974, he fired his manager, David Jonas, who then filed a law suit against Freddie. In December 1974, he sent his mother the fare to go to Puerto Rico and, in February 1975, the fare to come to Los Angeles. During that trip, Maria picked out the house that Freddie would buy for her and Karl in Los Angeles.

In March 1975, while performing at Lake Tahoe, Freddie met Kathy Barber, a divorced woman, whom he eventually married. Kathy got pregnant in June, and they were married in October. Freddie seemed withdrawn, and his mother felt he was not as open to her as in the past and drifting away from her.

Kathy went to a hypnotherapist, William Kroger, for help in natural childbirth, and Freddie began to see him to cure his drug addiction. In March 1976, Freddie's son, also called Freddie, was born, but by April there were problems with the marriage. Kathy was especially unhappy with his drug abuse.

By November, Freddie was distressed, depressed, confused, and exhausted. Also angry — he fired his gun recklessly at times and dislocated his wrist by hitting a wall with it. The legal battle with his manager continued (the contract was held to be valid by the court for the next three years), and he separated from Kathy, who then filed for divorce. He was arrested for driving while on drugs.

He described his state as a nervous breakdown. In October 1976, Dr. Kroger gave Freddie the MMPI, and the computer analysis described Freddie as possibly schizophrenic. It concluded by saying that his responses suggested a major emotional disorder and recommended professional evaluation. His fantasies were almost delusional. He was suspicious and paranoid, avoided close interpersonal relationships and was unable to express his emotions in modulated ways. The report described him as disoriented, perplexed, hostile, negativistic and suspicious. He was described as sensitive to criticism, ready to blame others, and likely to misinterpret the actions of others.

During December 1976 and January 1977, Freddie's condition worsened. At various times, his producer, Jimmy Komack, and his hypnotherapist, William Kroger, removed his drugs and his gun. Each time he demanded them back. His secretary described him as sinking deeper into depression. Off quaaludes he was manic; on them he was depressed.

His weight had dropped from 204 pounds to 165 pounds, and he had chronic diarrhoea. He told his father he was bleeding internally. On January 19, 1977, Freddie performed at the pre-inaugural ball for President Jimmy Carter.

Back in Los Angeles, he received the divorce agreement from Kathy's lawyers. During the early hours of January 29, he called Kathy at 12.15 am (it was her birthday) and spoke to her for a few minutes. His secretary was with him, and at Dr. Kroger arrived 1.15 am. After they left, Freddie called his financial manager, Dusty Snyder, who went to be with Freddie. Freddie shot himself in the head in front of Dusty. Thirty-three hours later he was declared dead.

12. MARILYN MONROE:

A SUICIDAL CAREER

The life and death of Marilyn Monroe continues to fascinate Americans. Interest seems to grow with each year, and many biographies have been written. Biographers have reported very little on her father's relatives. But her maternal grandparents were both psychiatrically disturbed. Her grandmother, Della Hogan, was chronically depressed, and her grandfather was mentally unstable. Both died insane. Della was hospitalized at Norwalk State Hospital in August 1927, fourteen months after Marilyn's birth, and died there nineteen days later of a heart attack during a manic episode.

Marilyn's mother, Gladys Monroe was born in 1900. Gladys was separated from her husband Martin Mortensen when she got pregnant by Stanley Gifford. Gifford's refusal to marry her or take care of her and the baby brought on a profound depression, the first of many in her life.

When Marilyn was seven, Gladys was hospitalized, eventually ending up at Norwalk State Hospital, like her own mother, Della. She remained hospitalized for most of her life and outlived Marilyn. Marilyn perhaps lived in fear of the genes that made her mother and grandmother mentally ill. Were those genes passed on to her and would they lead her also to end her days in a mental hospital?

Gladys decided not to take care of her baby, whom she named Norma Jeane. Instead, Marilyn was boarded with a family, the Bolenders, across the street from her grandmother. Gladys visited Marilyn regularly on weekends and took care of her once when she got whooping cough. The Bolenders had an adopted son,

Lester, and the two kids were quite close. Marilyn used to call Mr. Bolender her father. At this point in her life, Marilyn seems to have been a lively, curious and adventurous child. The major loss was when her dog, Tippy, was run over.

When Marilyn was seven, Gladys decided to take over the care of her daughter. She bought a house, rented it to a British couple and then rented back a couple of rooms for herself and Marilyn. Marilyn's life became much freer now. She was able to indulge in her love of movies, and she went to them whenever she could. She also fantasized about her missing father a great deal.

After Marilyn had been living with her mother for just over six months, Gladys was hospitalized for depression. (She was taken away while Marilyn was at school.) Marilyn stayed with the British couple for about a year and then, after they left the country, with neighbors, the Giffens. Gladys named a friend, Grace McKee, as Marilyn's guardian and refused to let the Giffens (who had three kids) adopt Marilyn. When the Giffens moved, Marilyn, now eleven, went to the Los Angeles Orphans' Home Society, where she stayed for twenty one months. Her guardian, Grace, visited her regularly there.

Eventually, Grace married and rescued Marilyn from the orphanage. However, she placed Marilyn in two foster homes briefly before bringing her home early in 1938. In her new home, Marilyn had three other children for companionship and became friendly with one, Beebe, who was two years younger than Marilyn. Here, Marilyn also became close to Grace's Aunt Ana, a widow, to whom she remained close until Ana's death ten years later. Ana introduced Marilyn to Christian Science.

The Goddards were neighbors to the Doughertys who had a son, Jim, about five years older than Marilyn.

The stories about the development of the relationship between Jim and Marilyn conflict. Certainly, Jim picked Marilyn and Beebe up after school and drove them home. He took Marilyn to the high school dance. Certainly the Goddards planned to move to West Virginia, and Gladys would not let her daughter go with them. At this time, Marilyn was living with Aunt Ana who perhaps saw the seductive ways of the young Marilyn and thought it a good idea to get her safely married. Jim and Marilyn married on June 19, 1942. Marilyn was sixteen and Jim was twenty-one. The evidence indicates that they loved each other sincerely and had a good marriage for the first few years.

These first sixteen years have several noteworthy features. Clearly, Marilyn's life had been chaotic and unpredictable. Who would keep her and for how long? Would she be put in a orphanage? Would her mother take care of her or would Gladys go crazy and leave her? Who was her father and where was he? How much loss would she suffer? First the Bolenders left, then her mother, the British couple, the Giffens, and now the Goddards. As soon as you got close to someone, they left. Even her dog was run over. Was she loved? Was she liked? If she was likable and lovable, maybe her father wouldn't have disappeared, maybe one of those families would have kept her, and maybe she wouldn't have to had to go into the orphanage.

The two factors most critical for a child are to have a safe and predictable world and to be loved and liked for yourself. Marilyn had neither, but at least now she had a loving husband.

The First Marriage: Transition Years

Marilyn's marriage to Jim Dougherty was reasonably happy. For the first couple of years Jim worked and, since he didn't want Marilyn to work, she stayed home. Marilyn was happy and came to enjoy love making.

However, she still found the attention of other men rewarding, and this would make Jim jealous. Eventually Jim decided he wanted to join the service, and Marilyn was distraught over this. He joined the Merchant Marine as a compromise and, as his initial posting was to Catalina, they lived together. But then Jim asked to be shipped overseas. His first tour kept him away for one year. Marilyn was probably faithful during this leave.

His first leave was wonderful. Interestingly, just before Jim was due back, Marilyn called her father (Gifford) who hung up on her. Jim's second departure was more upsetting than his first, and Marilyn moved from staying with her in-laws to staying with Aunt Ana. During the two years he was away, Marilyn wrote him about two hundred letters. (Yet years later, she claimed it was a marriage of convenience!)

After his first tour, she began work in a factory, and an Army photographer, David Conover, noticed her in the plant and encouraged her to begin a career as a model, with Aunt Ana's encouragement too. (Marilyn may have slept with Conover.) By the time Jim returned from his second tour, Marilyn was busy with her career as a model and had disengaged from Jim sexually and emotionally. He refused to leave the service, and she refused to stop her modelling career.

This episode is interesting. Jim must have known that he would lose his attractive and flirtatious wife if he went off to sea. Yet he went. Marilyn was abandoned by her first love and lover. She was described as distraught by his first departure and even more by his second. The loss must have recapitulated all of the other losses and leave-takings she had experienced as a child. One wonders. If Jim hadn't left and if he had encouraged her career, would her life course have been different?

Marilyn's Career

Marilyn was successful as a model, and she set out to break into movies. She began by divorcing Jim in

Nevada (in May 1946) since movie studios did not like married women. She started with Twentieth Century Fox (where she chose the name Marilyn Monroe) and began the stress of trying to build a career in movies.

She was cut by Twentieth Century Fox after two six-month contracts and by Columbia after one. She, like others, called her agent all the time, hoping for a part or an engagement, dealing with the disappointments of having nothing to do or getting only minor assignments. She was poor. In 1948 she fell in love with Freddie Karger, but he would not marry her. However, she did remain close to him and his family. In that year Aunt Ana died. Marilyn lost an important mother figure, but found another in Natasha Lytess, the head drama coach at Columbia. Marilyn lived with Natasha for a while and worked on her acting skills with Natasha's guidance.

Marilyn was taken over by Johnny Hyde, a good agent, who devoted the last few years of his life to establishing Marilyn's career. Marilyn moved from Natasha's to Johnny's house and became his lover. He wanted to marry her, but she told him that, though she loved him, she was not in love with him.

By the time he died in 1950, Johnny had persuaded Twentieth Century Fox to give Marilyn a seven-year contract, and she had two good roles (in The Asphalt Jungle and All About Eve). However, when he died, his family ordered her out of his house, and she went back to Natasha's. She was very depressed and took an overdose of thirty Nembutal tablets, but she was discovered and rescued by Natasha.

Twentieth Century Fox wanted Marilyn to be a sexual figure in movies. Natasha saw greater acting ability and wanted Marilyn to search for better roles. Yet Marilyn doubted her ability. Marilyn continually took lessons to improve her skills, with Natasha, with Lotte Goslar to learn mime, and with Michael Chekhov and

Lee Strasberg to improve her acting. Yet she needed her coach with her all the time, especially on the movie set. First Natasha and then Paula Strasberg accompanied her all the time, continually coaching and reassuring her.

In 1950, Marilyn had plastic surgery on her nose and chin. (She had previously used a retainer to pull in her front teeth a little and had switched from dirty to light blonde.)

By the end of 1951, Marilyn was becoming well known. She had met and become attracted to Arthur Miller (who was married and lived on the East Coast). Again, she tracked down her father and tried to visit him, and again he refused to see her. In 1951 too, Marilyn's lateness began to become a problem. She became increasingly concerned about her looks and would take two hours or more in front of her dressing room mirror trying to perfect her appearance before coming out. Natasha had destroyed Marilyn's trust by tricking her on two occasions financially, but Marilyn continued to be dependent upon her presence as a coach.

In 1952, Marilyn met Joe DiMaggio. They had little in common and had a stormy relationship. She was doubtful about marrying him, but finally did so in January 1954. The marriage was over by September 1954. He opposed her career, objected to her public sexuality, and was violent on occasion. Marilyn was very upset at the breakup but remained committed to her career. If marriage to Jim and now to Joe meant that she would have to leave her career, then marriage was out. Her career would go on. She started an independent company (Marilyn Monroe Productions) to purchase and produce films for her.

By the end of 1954, Marilyn had made other changes in addition to her break with Joe. Natasha was replaced by Paula Strasberg as her coach on location. She decided to leave Hollywood and move to New York City (which facilitated her relationship with Arthur Miller), began to study with Lee Strasberg and entered psychoanalysis with Marianne Kris.

She was also well established as a star (appearing in The Seven Year Itch), and becoming much more assertive about the films she made. Her new contract with Twentieth Century Fox greatly increased her pay and gave her control over the choice of directors.

She moved back to Hollywood, living with Milton Greene and his wife. (Milton Greene was her business partner in Marilyn Monroe Productions). Miller divorced his wife in 1956 and married Marilyn.

Marriage To Miller And The Decline

Soon after her marriage to Arthur Miller, Marilyn and Miller went to Great Britain to make a film directed by Lawrence Olivier. Miller was in conflict with Milton Greene (Marilyn's business partner) and Paula Strasberg (her coach), and he wrote critical things about Marilyn in his journal which she found. After Marilyn read Miller's comments on her, she was distraught, and her psychoanalyst flew over from New York to help calm her down.

In the years of marriage to Miller, Marilyn had two miscarriages and made several suicide attempts. The first was in the autumn of 1957 with barbiturates, but Miller was at home so that he was able to send for medical assistance for her.

She made two movies (Some Like It Hot and Let's Make Love), but she was becoming increasingly difficult to direct in movies. She was anxious about being on camera and angry with people connected with the movie. She was often late to the set and temperamental as are many stars. However, in 1959 she received minor awards for acting (from France and Italy) and performed with the classes at Lee

Strassberg's Acting Studio. But by 1960, Miller had virtually stopped writing and was spending his time trying to keep Marilyn together.

During the making of Let's Make Love, Marilyn had an affair with her co-star Yves Montand. For much of the time Miller and Simone Signoret (Montand's wife) were away, giving Marilyn and Montand freedom. When Miller eventually flew back to Los Angeles, it was clear that the marriage was over. But Marilyn and Miller agreed to stay together while his screenplay, The Misfits, was filmed with Marilyn in the lead.

During the shooting of the movie, Marilyn was taking uppers (Benzedrine) and downers (Nembutal). She spent sleepless nights, screaming at Miller, or drugged. Her lateness on the set continued. At one point, she was flown to Los Angeles under the supervision of her psychiatrist Ralph Greenson to withdraw from Nembutal and to switch to a milder drug.

As soon as the movie was finished, Miller moved out of Marilyn's Los Angeles house, and they disentangled their possessions in New York and Connecticut too. Clark Gable, Marilyn's co-star in The Misfits, died soon after the shooting was over, and his wife blamed his heart attack on the stress of working with Marilyn.

Back in New York, Marilyn was emotionally and physically ill. She tried to persuade herself to jump out of the window of her apartment (but failed), and her analyst in New York hospitalized her in the Payne Whitney Clinic. The clinic horrified Marilyn, especially her status as a suicide risk and the presence of other disturbed patients. She eventually managed to call Joe DiMaggio who checked her out and moved her to Columbia Presbyterian Hospital.

Returning to Los Angeles in 1961, she began to rely on her psychoanalyst there, Ralph Greenson. He invited Marilyn to come and live with his family and when she declined, had a friend of his, Eunice Murray, become her housekeeper. In May and June she had minor surgery (to remove her gall bladder and part of her pancreas). She was befriended by the "Rat Pack", a group including Frank Sinatra and Peter Lawford, and they moved Marilyn into the social life of the Kennedy's. She had an affair with John Kennedy and later became involved with and very attached to Robert Kennedy.

In 1962, she bought a small house, similar in style to Greenson's and moved in. She continued to visit New York (where she saw her New York psychoanalyst and John Kennedy). In April shooting began on Something's Got To Give, and Marilyn became Robert Kennedy's lover. However, her inability to work on the set led to her being fired by Twentieth Century Fox.

In July, Marilyn had an abortion and was very depressed. She began to see Greenson daily. In July, too, Robert Kennedy began to disengage himself from his relationship with her. Marilyn killed herself early on Sunday morning, August 5th, with an overdose of Nembutal and chloral hydrate. Greenson had visited her on Saturday night, and Eunice Murray had stayed over. Robert Kennedy was visiting San Francisco with his family that weekend. There is speculation that Robert Kennedy visited her that Saturday, that the Kennedy's had Marilyn killed and that the Mafia had her killed. But perhaps it doesn't matter what really happened in her final weekend. Marilyn was disintegrating rapidly. It is hard to imagine that she could have survived much longer

The Reasons Why Marilyn Committed Suicide

Family Disturbance

The mental illness in Marilyn's mother and maternal grandparents suggests that Marilyn may have had an affective psychiatric illness with a genetic basis. Of course, the existence of psychiatrically disturbed parents does not prove a genetic cause for the disturbance. Crazy parents create a disturbed childhood experience for their children as well as passing on their genes. However, Gladys seems to have done both. The childhood she created for Marilyn was the worst possible kind for someone with a genetic predisposition to depression.

What is especially noteworthy is that Marilyn lived with the fear that she would end up disturbed like her mother and grandmother. So her fear of becoming crazy may have been as potent a factor in her eventual disintegration as the actual genes that she may have inherited.

Marilyn's Disturbance

Interestingly, Marilyn appears to have few psychiatric symptoms in her early years. Only a mild stutter and painful menstrual periods are noted. In adulthood, there is evidence of headaches, excessive alcohol intake and drug abuse (especially uppers and downers). There is a history of depressive episodes, most of them occurring soon after the loss of a love or lover, and attempts at suicide mostly when someone was close by. There are three psychiatric hospitalizations, one for drug abuse and two for depression.

Back in the 1950s and 1960s, there were few good psychiatric treatments for depression. Antidepressants were not readily available, and Marilyn was spared electroconvulsive therapy. Marilyn's depression remained untreated. We do not know what type of psychotherapy was conducted by her analysts Kris and Greenson and whether it was appropriate.

Mother And Father Figures

Marilyn had two major types of figures in her social network. To substitute for the mother she never had, Marilyn usually had a close relationship with a female, usually a coach or mentor, first Natasha Lytess and then Paula Strasberg. In childhood, there were a succession of mother figures, but only Aunt Ana seemed to have provided the basis for a good relationship (in particular, with no rejection).

Marilyn's missing father seriously affected her life choices. Her two attempts to contact her father, rejected by him each time, only fueled her feeling of deprivation. She would look for and be attracted to father figures, and there were a succession of them in her life: from Johnny Hyde her agent to Arthur Miller. But men, especially confronted with a woman whose sexuality is so prominent, can hardly expected to fulfill the role of a father.

The Search For Approval

Because the little girl Marilyn was shuttled around from family to family and abandoned by most of them, Marilyn probably concluded that she was not very likable or lovable. Thus, she entered into the common pattern of suppressing her real self and adopting a facade self that would get her approval.

For Marilyn, who developed physically quite early and who was very pretty, sexuality was an easy choice. Aunt Ana noted the tight clothes and seductive behavior in Marilyn's early teens. After her first marriage at age sixteen, Marilyn still needed the attention of men. If men responded to her, then perhaps she was all right, a likable and lovable person.

Unfortunately, if you attract the attention of men, you also stimulate their sexual desires. So many of the men eventually became her lovers. Toward the end of her life, especially with the Kennedys, we have to wonder whether John or Robert really cared about Marilyn. By then, she was disintegrating, chronically depressed and taking drugs heavily. Their relationship with her must have been based primarily upon her fame and availability for sexual intercourse.

Not only, therefore, would the men in her life disappoint her, by abusing her and abandoning her, but they would not provide the unconditional love that she needed immediately and had needed even more urgently as a child.

Marilyn adopted, therefore, the tactic of getting attention by her looks and sexual style. Her lateness may have been caused in part by her depression and drug abuse, but it was also a result of her insecurity (will people really like me?) and her reliance on her looks for attention.

She had her teeth straightened and minor plastic surgery and took incredible care getting ready for a social appearance. Marilyn's looks had to be perfect because the little girl she once was, the real Marilyn, was far from perfect as proved by all of those adults who abandoned her.

Marilyn's Emotional States

I have discussed Marilyn's depression and hinted at her insecurities. In all likelihood, she soon developed a fear of abandonment and the loss of love. She attempted suicide after losing Johnny Hyde and killed herself when Robert Kennedy was about to discard her. She could never trust people, and unfortunately her life experiences appeared to prove that she was right to distrust others.

Socially, she often appeared to be shy, especially in groups. She had a fear of meeting strangers (perhaps they would see her inadequacies?), and her directors and co-stars were aware of her insecurities as an actress. (It is interesting that she never appeared in a play on stage. She performed in only one or two scenes from plays at the Actor's Studio.)

There appears to have been strong inner anger that led to angry outbursts and displays of bad temper. At the end of her marriage with Arthur Miller, she spent nights screaming curses at him.

Clearly this inner anger stemmed from the anger at her mother and father for abandoning her. Every betrayal and desertion thereafter would feed into this anger, and it would be felt toward the new rejecting person and also be renewed toward her parents.

Distorting The Past

One habit of Marilyn is of particular interest because she shares it with Ernest Hemingway who also killed himself. Marilyn distorted the past. She claimed that her dog was killed by a neighbor. (It was run over accidentally). She claimed horrible mistreatments at the orphanage that appear to be false. When she was young she claimed that Clark Gable was her father. She claimed to have been smothered by her grandmother (but at an age when she could hardly have remembered) and raped by a boarder (except that she never lived with anyone who took in boarders).

Like Hemingway, Marilyn moved on, abandoning old friends and locales, and like him she distorted the past, making it usually worse than it was. Is it that she wanted to arouse sympathy or that she thought that Marilyn's real life was boring and needed embellishing?

Lack Of Education

Marilyn is described as being intelligent, but she was poorly educated, leaving school at sixteen. She seemed to have been bothered by this. She tried to read good literature, but Miller noted that she dipped into books and rarely finished them. She was shaky about the names of the authors and their characters.

Her lack of education may have added to her doubts about her worth. Having decided (consciously or unconsciously) to get attention by means of her looks and sexuality, she feared perhaps being seen as a dumb blonde. Yet her intellect was not developed.

Related to this, she had never received training as an actor. Here, however, she was willing to take classes, though she would become over-dependent upon her coach because of her self-doubt over her acting ability.

Social Resources

It is worth noting that Marilyn usually lived with or was very close to families, most of which gave her affection. (The list includes the Bollenders, Goddards, Doughertys, Kargers, DiMaggios, Greenes, Strasbergs, Millers, and Greensons.) She always had friends and affection. But none of these families and friends was enough. Because none of them could take the place of Mom and Dad.

Final Stresses

At the end of her life, Marilyn had lost her job. She had been fired from a movie for the first time. She was about to lose her current lover, Robert Kennedy. Her addiction to drugs was greater than ever and her depression as bad. She had analysts in Los Angeles and New York to respond to her needs daily. (She seems to have been terrified to be without a therapist close at hand.)

What was in store for her? The decline of her fame as a movie star. Abandonment by her lovers. Aging was making it more difficult to appear in public as beautiful as she once thought she was. Marilyn was nothing but a beautiful woman on screen and an attractive sexual object in bed. Age changes that.

Marilyn was close to the end of her life as she defined it. She had arrived at an existential choice point. To create a new existence or to end the old one. She chose to end the old one.

13. VINCENT VAN GOGH:

THE SECOND VINCENT

Vincent Van Gogh's parents lived in Zundert, in the Netherlands, where his father, Theodorus, was a pastor. Theodorus and his wife, Anna, had a stillborn son. They registered the birth, named the child Vincent after his grandfather, and buried him in the graveyard at Zundert.

Anna grieved a lot over the death of the baby. She wondered whether the death of her child was a punishment for her sins. Within a year, in 1853, Anna was pregnant again, but Anna was fearful that this child, too, would be born dead. She waited for the birth with foreboding.

The child was born on March 30, 1853. He had red hair and freckles, with blue-green eyes. He was born exactly one year to the day after the dead Vincent, the number of his birth certificate was the same (twenty-nine), and his parents named him Vincent also. Vincent was followed by a sister Anna two years later, and then Theo, Elizabeth, Wilhelmien and Cornelius.

Vincent grew up lonely and isolated. Anna was preoccupied with her subsequent pregnancies and babies. She seemed not to like him and rarely showed him any warmth. His father had little understanding of people in general and was no help to his son.

Vincent had been named after his dead brother, and every Sunday, his mother marched the children off to the graveyard to put flowers on the dead child's grave. Vincent grew up feeling unloved and rejected and constantly reminded that his mother wanted the first Vincent and not this second one who came later.

Vincent soon developed his mother's quick temper and nervousness. He would defy his mother and seemed almost to enjoy provoking her. For example, he played with the rough lads in the village against his mother's wishes, and he took little interest in being clean or tidy. His speech was rough sounding and spasmodic. However, he admired his father, enjoying the sermons and accompanying him on his parish duties, and he soon decided that he too wanted to become a pastor.

As a child, Vincent spent a lot of time by himself, wandering the countryside, and he developed an early interest in drawing. (His mother, though good at drawing herself, gave him no advice or encouragement.) Vincent shared a bed with his younger brother Theo, who worshipped Vincent, and the two grew very close. Vincent had an uncle, also called Vincent, who was an art dealer and who, when he visited, seemed to like Vincent and take an interest in him.

When he was eleven, Vincent was sent to a boarding school, but he felt out of place there. He was loutish compared to the other boys, and his speech was almost a stammer. The other boys disliked him, and Vincent withdrew from them after his initial efforts to be friendly, even eating by himself in a corner of the dining room. Vincent spent five years at the school and did not make one close friend.

While there, however, he did acquire a love for reading, and he continued his drawing. But his loneliness made him hostile, and his hostility increased his rejection by others. He was argumentative with his fellow students and with his teachers.

Vincent left school at the age of sixteen. His parents ignored his wish to become a pastor like his father, and Uncle Vincent got him a job in an art gallery. Vincent did not protest and left in the summer of 1869 for The Hague.

Once there, Vincent changed his style a little,

dressing neatly and keeping tidy, though he still looked like a peasant. He was unattractive, with spasmodic speech. Separated from his brother Theo, he began his habit of writing regularly to him. He would often include sketches to Theo, but though he drew and worked in art galleries for several years, Vincent did not recognize that he had a talent for art. He still hoped one day to become a pastor.

In 1873 when Vincent was twenty, his firm transferred him to London. Vincent visited the art galleries and museums of London and kept sketching. However, he also read the Bible a great deal and went to church often. He became quite friendly with the family with whom he was lodging, a French family who ran a boarding school. Vincent, now twenty-one, helped with the boys. The family had a daughter, Ursula, with whom Vincent fell in love, but when he finally found the courage to tell her of his love, she rejected him coldly. Vincent would not accept her rejection, and he continued to pester her until the family asked him to leave.

After a vacation back home in the Netherlands, his family sent his sister Anna to accompany him back to London. Anna got a job as a teacher at a girl's school and, when she saw how miserable Vincent was in London after his rejection by Ursula and how bad tempered he was at work, she persuaded their mother to get him transferred to Paris. Vincent was furious over his mother's interference and so difficult that he was transferred back to London after two months. But the London branch could tolerate him no longer, so they sent him back to Paris. After Christmas, 1875, the art gallery and Vincent could no longer tolerate each other, and so they parted company.

On the day he finally left the firm, Vincent received a letter from the principal of a boys school in England offering Vincent a month's trial. In the spring of 1876,

Vincent arrived to find the school moving from Ramsgate to London. The school would not pay his fare, so Vincent walked there, taking two days. The school then told him that they had no salary for him. Vincent tried to get a job as a missionary for the poor in London, but he was turned down because he was too young. He heard that a Methodist minister needed an assistant, and Vincent got the position. Vincent was at last close to realizing his dream, teaching Bible School and occasionally preaching. Even though he was unpaid and often hungry, Vincent was happy.

From Preacher To Painter

The congregation found Vincent's accent and stammering speech difficult to follow, but he drove himself until his health collapsed. He decided to return home for Christmas and he arrived thin and haggard, clothes in rags, sick and exhausted.

Uncle Vincent came to the rescue again and found him a job with a bookseller in Dordrecht in the Netherlands. Vincent started there in January 1877. But after three months Vincent quit to begin training in Amsterdam for the ministry.

Vincent's personal style soon alienated his teachers. They decided that he would never pass the examinations, and Vincent quit after a year. The minister Vincent had worked for briefly in London helped Vincent gain admission to a training program for missionaries, but again Vincent's style led the school to refuse to graduate him. Vincent's father appealed to the program to let Vincent work for them for free. They agreed, and Vincent went off to Le Borinage, a mining area in the south of Belgium in December 1878.

He worked well there and by January was given a salary for a six-month trial. Vincent, however, showed a lack of self-control. He moved into a shabby hut and gave away everything he had. He lived worse than the miners he was supposed to minister to, and his superiors ordered him to dress and behave like a proper missionary. He refused and in July was given three months to find another position.

Finally, Vincent reflected. He liked working with the poor people at Le Borinage, but he had failed at every career he had tried. What if he tried drawing? He returned to Le Borinage and, subsisting on a little money sent to him from time to time by his family, sketched the peasants.

Vincent's life as painter from 1879 until his death was marked by poverty. He rarely had enough money to buy food or to pay people to model for his painting. His paintings were not popular, and his brother Theo had difficulty selling any of them. However, his work was also characterized by a driven quality so that he painted and painted and neglected all other activities. Even if Vincent had had sufficient money, he still would have neglected his diet.

Vincent continued to have difficulty getting along with others: fellow painters, his family, and the instructors at art institutes where he enrolled for classes. Vincent wandered from Paris, to Brussels, to little towns like Drenthe, and back home where as usual he got into fights with his parents about his life style.

Vincent's Loves

Vincent had fallen in love with Ursula Loyer, the daughter of his landlord in London, without her being aware of it. In 1881, a similar incident happened while he was living at home with his parents. A cousin, Kee Vos, who was widowed with a son, came to stay, and Vincent fell in love with her. When he finally screwed up the courage to tell her of his love, she was horrified and rejected him. As before, he pursued her even though it was clear that she could not stand him.

He followed her to Amsterdam, where her parents

refused to let him see her. In frustration, he put his hand into the flame of an oil lamp, demanding to see her. They maintained their refusal. Although Vincent's lifestyle can be seen as self-destructive in a very general sense, and his neglect of his food and health was damaging to him, this was the first incident of a deliberate impulsive act of self-harm.

In 1882, Vincent moved to The Hague and worked with a painter there, Anton Mauve. Missing Kee, he met a vagrant, Christine, who drifted around with her mother, and moved them into his apartment. He decided that he was in love with Christine and that she would be his wife. Soon, however, Christine grew to dislike Vincent's ways, and she walked out on him.

In 1884, Vincent was again back with his parents, having nursed his mother through her recovery from a broken hip. The family next door had a daughter in her forties, ten years older than Vincent, shy, plain and never married. Gradually Vincent and she became friendly and fell in love. This time, Vincent's love was appropriate, and it was returned. But when Vincent asked Margot's father for permission to marry her, he refused. Margot attempted suicide with poison, and her family sent her away and refused to let Vincent ever see her again. This time, the failure was not Vincent's fault, but rather that fault of Margot's possessive parents. Vincent's parents, who had suffered a lot from their son's lifestyle, did not sympathize with him at all in this crisis.

The End

Vincent's father died in 1885, and soon the villagers told Vincent to leave. Vincent again wandered from town to town. He was thirty-three and had sold no paintings, only a few drawings.

His health began to get worse. During a six week period in Paris, for example, he ate only three hot meals containing meat. He smoked to dampen his hunger and tried to get by on bread and coffee. He had pains in his abdomen, and his teeth broke. He slept little and suffered from headaches and nightmares. He feared a breakdown but did little to prevent one.

In 1886 he moved in with his brother Theo in Paris (and it was at this point that Vincent bought himself a revolver, as had most of his fellow art students). After one argument between the art students and the instructors, Vincent went home to get his revolver to kill the director of the art school, but when he returned the director had left.

During the next year, Vincent began to drink more. He quarreled with everyone and was frequently in trouble with the gendarmes. The painter Paul Gauguin was back in Paris, and Vincent tried to persuade Gauguin to move to the south of France with him and set up a school of painting.

At first Gauguin refused, and so with Theo's aid Vincent moved to Arles by himself. He was happy there at first, though his lonely life style continued, together with his neglect of food and sleep. The people of the town thought him very odd and refused to pose as models for him. Eventually he became exhausted, and he developed terrible headaches and stomach pains.

Theo finally persuaded Gauguin to go and join Vincent in Arles, and after many delays Gauguin arrived in October 1888. Gauguin was clean and fastidious. Under his guidance, the studio was cleaned, and meals were regular. But soon Vincent and Gauguin began quarreling, mostly about art and painters. Gauguin claimed to have woken up in the night twice to find Vincent creeping toward his bed. Gauguin considered returning to Paris, and by Christmas, Gauguin was determined to leave. Two days before Christmas, Gauguin was out on the street when he turned to find Vincent coming at him holding an open razor. Vincent fled to the studio, whereupon he cut off part of his right ear. He tied a scarf around his head to stem the bleeding, put the piece of severed ear in an envelope and gave it to a girl whom he knew slightly.

After his hospitalization, living alone, his exhaustion returned. He began to have hallucinations and to think that the people in the town were persecuting him. (In fact, the children and even the adults did jeer at him and harass him.) In February he was hospitalized again and soon a third time. In May 1889 he agreed with his doctors to move to an asylum in the neighboring town of Saint-Remy.

While there, Vincent continued to paint and, surrounded by psychiatric patients, he lost his fear of madness. In April 1890, Vincent went back to Paris, where Theo had found him lodgings in the nearby town of Auvers with a heart specialist named Gachet who was interested in art.

Theo was now married, had a child and was preoccupied with his own affairs, which upset Vincent. He began to quarrel with Gachet and, after one fight, he pulled his revolver out, aimed it at Gachet, but did not fire it. He went back to his rooms and wrote a letter to his brother, walked out into the countryside and shot himself.

The bullet entered his abdomen, and Vincent was able to stagger back to his rooms. Theo arrived the next day to be with Vincent, who died the next morning, July 29, 1890, at the age of thirty-seven.

Discussion

It is easy to classify Vincent as psychiatrically disturbed but difficult, looking back a hundred years later, to diagnose him accurately, though many modern psychiatrists have tried to decide which psychiatric label best fits Vincent. For most of his life, Vincent was a loner, difficult to get along with, with a seemingly uncontrollable temper (though perhaps Vincent chose not to control it). In all of his activities, he seemed driven, neglecting his health and welfare simply to preach or to paint.

We call a chronic maladaptive life style a personality disorder, and Vincent clearly had, at the very least, such a disorder. Vincent was angry. He quarreled with everyone, but because of his inferior status in life, most of those he quarreled with were his superiors or, eventually, his rivals in the art world. Where does this anger have its roots? In his childhood, of course.

Vincent was treated cruelly by his parents, and especially by his mother. She was too preoccupied with her own guilt and depression and her subsequent children to provide Vincent with the love he needed. She constructed a life for him in which he could feel only that he was an unworthy replacement for the elder brother, dead at birth, whom his mother really wanted. Vincent was led believe that he had no right to exist.

So this anger, rightfully felt toward his mother, expressed itself as childhood rebellion, developing into anger at any authority figure. It is interesting that he remained so dependent upon his parents. Children who develop a healthy sense of self eventually disengage themselves from such pathological parents. But Vincent always came back. As a teenager, in his twenties and in his thirties, he returned home to quarrel.

Yet Vincent was not devoid of social skills and relationships. Theo loved him and perhaps his other siblings had some positive feelings for him. Margot, the neighbour with whom he fell in love, might have made him a good companion. But his mother had betrayed his trust as an infant. How could he trust anyone now?

Vincent's self-esteem must have been low. Unwanted as a child, not encouraged in anything he tried to do, a failure as a preacher, rejected by women he loved, ridiculed and persecuted by neighbours, and a failure (at least in his life-time) as a painter, Vincent accomplished nothing that brought him praise, love or any kind of reward. Theo loved him. And his paintings were good. But no one thought his art worth purchasing.

Toward the end of his life, he may have become psychotic. Possibly he had delusions and hallucinations. Certainly he was put in an asylum.

Vincent's suicide (and indeed his self-mutilation at Arles earlier) were both after he had been about to attack someone else. Each time, his attack was aborted when he confronted the person. Each time, the person was only the most recent irritant in his life. The Freudian view of suicide is that it is anger felt toward someone else, suppressed or repressed and directed against the self. Vincent's anger at his parents was expressed toward them, but perhaps never sufficiently to be satisfying. The anger toward his peers and superiors was expressed verbally, but again perhaps never sufficiently to be cathartic. The well of anger was still full, and Vincent had a life-style that made him enemies and caused him frustrations that kept filling up the well of anger. Perhaps Vincent feared that he would one day indeed kill someone, and he killed himself for fear of that?

In one way, Vincent is the saddest of the famous suicides for most of the others were accorded some recognition for their talent during their life time, and some were even recognized as exceptional. Vincent's incredible talent was recognized only after his death.

14. WILLIAM INGE:

HOMOSEXUAL PLAYWRIGHT

William Inge was born on May 3, 1913, in
Independence, Kansas, the fifth and last child of the
family. His father was a traveling salesman who was
absent a good deal, and he was raised primarily by his
mother, a neurasthenic woman. He became a Momma's
boy, was teased as a sissy by boys at school, did not date
much in high school, and became a homosexual. He
never publicly admitted being a homosexual, but he
hinted at it in his writing.

He liked recitation as a child, and at high school he
enjoyed acting and cheerleading. He got an
undergraduate degree from the University of Kansas in
1935 where he acted and studied drama. He spent the
summers acting in touring vaudeville shows, and he
intended to become an actor when he graduated.
However, the uncertainties of the profession and the
likelihood of failure in trying to become a great actor led
him to accept a scholarship for graduate study at
George Peabody College.

His regret over his choice led him to quit two weeks
before the end of his course of study. He returned home
to work as a laborer on a highway crew, a scriptwriter
and announcer for the local radio station, and finally a
teacher of English in a local high school. He found to his
surprise that he liked teaching, and so he returned to
George Peabody College in the summer of 1938 to finish
his Master's degree. He then became an Instructor at
Stephens College in Columbia, Missouri.

At Stephens College, one of his colleagues was a
former actress, and she renewed his interest in theater.
But he was depressed, drinking heavily, and had a
nervous breakdown. He began to write both for

pleasure and to release his tensions which improved his writing skills and gave him confidence. In 1943, he accepted a job as drama critic for the St. Louis Star-Times, replacing a friend who had gone off to war. He also became friends with Tennessee Williams who encouraged Inge to write plays.

When his friend returned from the war, Inge had to give up his job, and he took a position at Washington University in St. Louis. He hated the job, and Tennessee Williams introduced Inge to Margo Jones who produced plays in Dallas. She put on Inge's first play, and the response was encouraging enough that Inge continued to write while teaching at Washington University. He also continued to drink heavily, joining Alcoholics Anonymous in 1948 but never really overcoming the addiction. In 1949, his play Come Back Little Sheba was produced on Broadway and was so successful that Inge never had to teach again.

In the 1950s, all of his plays were both critical and commercial successes. "Picnic" won a Pulitzer Prize, and he earned over a million dollars from his plays and the films that were made from them. Nevertheless, his depressions and alcoholism continued. He entered psychoanalysis which seemed to help him a little, but he never could accept his own homosexuality, and he certainly never acknowledged it in the way Tennessee Williams did.

In the 1960s, Inge used some of his own money to produce his new plays which were not well received. Inge had three successive plays fail on Broadway, and he never tried again. The criticism hurt him a great deal, but the films from his earlier plays were successes. He won an Oscar for the screenplay of Splendor in the Grass.

Inge spent the last years of his life in California where he continued to write and to advise the theater workshops at UCLA. He wrote two plays which were performed on the West Coast but never published. He wrote two novels, neither of which was widely acclaimed. He lived his final few years with his widowed sister in Los Angeles who shielded him from interviewers. A few days before his suicide, Inge said that life had always been very ugly to him and that he wanted to write about loneliness and ineffectuality.

Inge attempted to kill himself with barbiturates on June 2 1973. The hospital sent him to the psychiatric unit, but he signed himself out the next day. On June 10, his sister found him dead in the garage at 4.30 am, sitting in his Mercedes-Benz with the engine running.

15. SIGMUND FREUD:

AN ASSISTED-SUICIDE

The life and work of Sigmund Freud are well known — a neurologist who became interested in the human mind and proposed a theory, called psychoanalytic theory, to explain how the mind affects our behavior. His life is not very remarkable — the diligent life of a scholar — except that in his death he anticipated a major controversy of modern times. In 1938, Freud asked his physician to inject him with a lethal dose of morphine. Freud was one of the first physician-assisted suicides, and his physician anticipated Dr. Jack Kervorkian, today's "Doctor of Death," by fifty years.

Sigmund Freud was born as Sigismund Schlomo Freud on May 6, 1856, in the Moravian town of Freiberg now known as Pribor, Czechoslovakia. His father Jacob was a wool merchant who was never very wealthy. Jacob married his third wife, Amalia, in 1855 when he was forty, twenty years older than her. Two grown-up sons from his first marriage lived nearby, and Freud grew up playing with his nephew who was one year older than himself. In 1859, the family moved to Leipzig and the next year to Vienna. Freud remained in Vienna, where he graduated from medical school, saw patients and developed his theory. By the early 1900s he was internationally known for his theories of the mind.

Freud was diagnosed with cancer of the palate in 1923. The growth was removed, but the cancer continued to plague Freud until his death in 1939. Even in the 1920s, his physician noted his readiness for suicide. Freud made it clear that he wanted his physician to help him leave the world in a decent manner if his suffering should be intense and prolonged. Freud described his depression that year as the first of his life and, since he had been mildly depressed many times before, this depression must have been severe.

Freud later underwent over thirty operations and had scores of fittings, cleanings and refittings of a prosthesis for his jaw. He retrained himself to speak, but his voice never recovered its clarity. The operations also affected his hearing, making him almost deaf in his right ear. He no longer attended the psychoanalytic meetings partly because of these physical problems. Freud also developed occasional angina. His diary for November and December 1929 notes heart and intestinal problems, anti-semitic riots, and being passed over for the Nobel Prize.

His fame continued to grow, and honors were bestowed upon him. His ideas, albeit distorted, had permeated educated society around the world, and he was made an honorary member of many societies. Journals on psychoanalysis were formed in most major countries. Translations of his work appeared. Frankfurt awarded him the Goethe Prize for literature in 1930. But sad events also took place, such as the death of Karl Abraham, a colleague, in 1924 at the age of 48, followed by his card partners in Vienna with whom he had played tarok every Saturday night, his mother in 1930, and Sandor Ferenczi, another colleague, in 1933.

The rise of the Nazis in Germany led to further problems. Freud's works were included in public book burnings in May 1933. Although Freud considered going into exile, he resisted it until the German take-over of Austria in March 1938. During that Spring, over 500 Austrian Jews committed suicide. Freud rejected the idea of suicide, however, when it was raised by his daughter Anna. Himmler urged that the Freuds be imprisoned, but Goering and the German Foreign Office counseled prudence. Many years earlier, Freud had collaborated on a book on Woodrow Wilson with

William Bullit who was now the American Ambassador to France. Through his influence President Roosevelt instructed the American Ambassador in Berlin to watch over Freud's case. Freud refused exile until Anna was taken to the Gestapo headquarters on March 22, 1938. After that, with friends paying the ransom (Freud's bank accounts had been confiscated), Freud left Vienna on June 4, 1938, arriving in London on June 6.

In England, he remained weak but continued to see a few patients and to write. He underwent major surgery for his cancer in September and later had some radium treatment. By August 1939, the pain from the cancer was severe, and the smell from his ulcerated cancer was so bad that even his pet dog avoided from him. He was extremely weak, and it was hard to feed him, yet he rejected sedation.

On September 21, he reminded his physician (Max Schur, who had also gone into exile in London) of their agreement to end Freud's life in just these circumstances. Schur injected Freud with three centigrams of morphine on September 21, followed by two more injections the next day. Freud died at three in the morning on September 23, 1939.

Even at the point of his death, his relatives and friends reported nothing that would indicate psychiatric illness. He had lived as long as he could, and he chose to hasten his death just a little. Freud's suicide appears to the rational act of a rational person. It is interesting to note, however, the Freud himself proposed a theory of why people commit suicide, and his theory has no validity for his own suicidal death!

16. JOE ORTON AND KENNETH

HALLIWELL:

A MURDER-SUICIDE

Joe Orton was born on January 1, 1933, as John Orton, in a lower class housing estate in Leicester. His mother Elsie, worked as a machinist until her eyesight failed and she had to become a cleaning lady. His father William worked as a gardener for the local government. Joe was their first child — he had a younger brother and two younger sisters. The family was quite poor. They had no telephone, no car, and no appliances. One of Elsie's treasures was a cheap pink glass dish from Woolworths.

All the children remembered the home as unhappy. The parents bickered, and the home was drab and depressing. William had little to do with his children. Joe felt close to his mother, buying her birthday presents as a teenager, but not his father. (When he returned dutifully for his annual visit, he always brought Elsie gifts, but never lavished money on her as she had hoped. She died in 1966.) Elsie was often brutal to her children, beating them severely, on occasions until they were unconscious.

Elsie complained a lot about William, telling everyone she should never had married him. They never kissed, and once the fourth child was born, Elsie banished William to another room. After 1945, William never had sex again with his wife.

Joe had asthma as a child and missed school a lot because of illness. He reported his first sexual encounter at the age of fourteen when a man masturbated him in a movie theater. But Joe was interested in girls for a while during his adolescent years.

Elsie believed that Joe had gifts so, after Joe had failed the eleven-plus exam for entrance to a grammar school, she decided to send him to a private school, not realizing it was a commercial school. Joe attended the school from 1945 to 1947. Teachers there remember Joe as semi-literate and poor at expressing himself in speech or in writing.

Somehow, though, Joe became interested in theater. He joined several local dramatic societies and was thrilled at any part he was given. He decided to try to enter the Royal Academy of Dramatic Art (RADA) and took elocution lessons to improve his diction and prepare for the examination. He even took jobs to try to save money for the tuition should he be accepted. However, he hated the low level jobs he got, and he was usually fired. Theater gave him his only success.

Joe auditioned at RADA in January, 1951 and was accepted. The town government helped out with the tuition. An attack of appendicitis delayed his arrival until May, 1951. It was there that he met Ken.

Kenneth Halliwell

Ken's father, Charles, was a chartered accountant. The family lived in a neat duplex near Liverpool. Ken was born on June 23, 1926, and his mother, Daisy, was told it would be too dangerous to have any more children. Ken grew up shy, keeping to himself. He read a lot and liked dressing up and acting. He developed into a mother's boy, always clinging to his mother when company was around. She pampered Ken and was close to him.

In September, 1937, Daisy was stung by a wasp and choked to death in front of Ken. Ken and his father were left together, but the relationship was cold and distant. His father ignored him, and Ken ran away from home many times.

Ken became interested in the theater and joined the local dramatic society in which he was very successful, much more so than Joe later. Although he went to grammar school, Ken stubbornly refused to go to University. From 1942 to 1951, he played prominent roles in twenty productions. In 1944, Ken became a conscientious objector and served in the coal mines at Wigan, Lancashire.

In 1949, Ken's father committed suicide by putting his head in the gas oven. Ken was twenty-three years old. He came downstairs, saw his father, stepped over the body and turned the gas off. After having his morning tea and a shave, he went next door to the neighbors to call the police.

He auditioned at RADA at the same time as Joe, but was rejected. Finally, he persuaded RADA to admit him, and he paid for his own tuition from the small sum of money his father had left him.

Life With Ken

Joe soon moved in with Ken, and they became lovers. In their two years at RADA, surprisingly, Joe did well and Ken poorly. Ken was inhibited and wooden on stage, far too anxious. Joe graduated while Ken received only a Certificate of Merit. Joe worked for a few months as an assistant stage manager but disliked the work. His contract was not renewed. Ken went off to work on the stage for a summer season in Wales, his only work as an actor.

They came back to London and lived together again. Writing was Ken's idea. Together they wrote several novels. Initially, Ken wrote and Joe typed. Gradually, Joe played a more important role, until their works were truly joint efforts. Because they had only Ken's inheritance to live on, they lived an ascetic life. They wrote during the day to limit the electric bill. For three years, they both worked for six months each year at a factory to earn enough to buy a new apartment. A publisher recalls a meal served by Ken of rice with sardines followed by rice with syrup.

Joe worked hard to develop his writing skills. He practiced with lists of words, sentences, and word constructions. They began to submit their work in 1955, but it was consistently rejected. However, Charles Montieth at Faber & Faber saw potential and encouraged them. He took them out to dinner and gave a party for them.

In 1957, Joe and Ken began also to write their own individual works, which also met with rejection. In 1958, Joe "invented" Mrs. Edna Welthorpe who wrote letters to the newspapers and to companies. In these letters, Joe was able to practice his writing skills and express his hostility. (In one of his first letters from Edna, she requested permission to use the local Baptist Church Hall for a performance of a play on homosexuals called The Pansy.) Joe's last novel, Head To Toe, was written in 1961 and published only after Joe's death.

In 1959, they started taking books from the public library, pasting in pictures incongruent with the content, writing obscene descriptions of the books and generally defacing them. The changes were funny, but they were also obscene and hostile. In 1962, Joe and Ken were arrested for this "crime," and they were sentenced to six months in prison, sentences they served in separate prisons. Ken was repentant after the prison time, but the experience seem to have given Joe a focus for his writing.

In 1962, Joe wrote a play, The Visit, which was praised by the British Broadcasting Company and the Royal Court Theater. Thus encouraged, Joe wrote The Ruffian On The Stair, which was accepted by the BBC in 1963. It was broadcast in August 1964 to excellent reviews. But by then, Entertaining Mr Sloane was already a success on stage, the Good And Faithful Servant completed and Loot underway. Of course, there were many crises in the production of the plays, and they often opened to bad reviews. But despite this, Joe's fame and prestige grew with each new project. Loot was judged the best play of 1966 by the Evening Standard, purchased for Broadway and sold to the movies.

During this period, Joe's success contrasted with Ken's failures. His manuscripts lay at home, rejected. Joe shrugged off his mother's death, while Ken had never recovered from his mother's death. Joe went around London with important people, while Ken stayed home alone. Joe made sexuality, isolation and rage the topics for his comic writing; Ken was oppressed by his sexuality, isolation and rage. Joe took the ideas he and Ken had created together in their earlier rejected work and now turned them into successful scripts, acknowledging Ken's contribution only in his diary, not in public.

The relationship between Joe and Ken began to deteriorate after Joe's success, and soon Joe wanted to extricate himself from the relationship. They bickered and fought. Ken was chronically depressed and jealous of Joe's success. He had gone bald in his twenties and was greatly embarrassed by his physical appearance. (One of the first things Joe had done with his money from writing was to buy Ken a toupee.) Ken disliked himself so much, he could not believe that anyone else could like him. When they went out together, Ken sulked in the background and was generally rude and hostile. Ken was never photographed and never mentioned. When they talked about breaking up, Ken often threatened suicide. Joe wanted to be free from this.

In 1951 when they met, Ken was masculine and assertive. After success came to Joe, Ken turned into a complaining housewife. Initially, it was Ken's inheritance from his father that had supported them. Now it was Joe's financial success from his plays that paid the bills. Joe was gone for much of the time. Whereas for most of their life together, they had been in each other's company almost all of the time, Joe now had rehearsals to attend, producers to meet, and all the other tasks associated with his profession.

Joe encouraged Ken with his attempts at painting. In 1967, Joe arranged a showing at a Chelsea art gallery. But there was no immediate success for Ken, for only Joe's business associates bought any pictures. In 1966, Ken sent a play to Joe's agent who rejected it. Having educated Joe and helped him develop his comic writing skills, Ken now had to face his own failure. He had failed as an actor, he had failed as a writer, and it looked as if he would continue to fail.

Interpersonally, Ken was an outcast. The circle of friends he and Joe had were almost all from Joe's career, and all of them found Ken unpleasant to have around. Ken had considered suicide for a long period. In 1953, at the RADA, he had told a fellow actress that he would probably end up like his father. In 1962 he had slashed his wrists. In a novel he wrote with Joe, The Boy Hairdresser, the character based on Ken contemplated suicide.

Meanwhile, Joe documented all of this and more in great detail in his daily diary which Ken read and re-read. Ken's only attempt at a solution was to urge a move out of London, to the suburbs or to Brighton. They did go down to Brighton to look at places, but Joe wanted to stay in London. The most he would consider was to visit Ken in Brighton on weekends. Joe could no longer stand sex with Ken, and Joe's friends were surprised at Joe's indifference to Ken's pain.

On their last vacation together, to Morocco, only six weeks before the deaths, Joe easily and casually had sex with a variety of Moroccan youths, while Ken was more timid. Although he was taking librium and valium, Ken remained anxious. Finally, three days before leaving for London, Ken physically attacked Joe.

Ken began to suffer from all kinds of physical complaints in 1967. After they had taken a miserable trip to Libya in March, Ken's depression deepened. Spots appeared on his legs, he had heart palpitations, and he had pains in his chest. He went to various doctors, until one told him that he was overly nervous and suffering from guilt over his mother's death and prescribed tranquilizers.

Back in London on June 30, Ken came down with hay fever. Joe finished What The Butler Saw in early July, and Ken read it. He made some suggestions which Joe liked and saw that it would be a great success. At a party on July 21, a television producer told Ken that people disliked him and that he was a middle-aged nonentity. Ken was stunned and dejected, but he continued to bore people with his stories of Joe's casual sexual promiscuity and his psychosomatic complaints. The more Ken needed love, the more he made himself unlovable. The only way left to Ken to make his presence felt, of proving to himself, to Joe and to the world that he mattered was to murder.

In April, Ken had been urged to seek help and had visited a Dr. Douglas Ismay, a general practitioner. By August 3 Ken was acutely suicidal. He visited the suicide prevention center run by the Samaritans. They gave him an appointment for some future time, and so he visited Dr. Ismay without an appointment. Dr. Ismay gave him antidepressants and amphetamines. Ken went back to Dr. Ismay on August 4 and called him in desperation on August 8. Dr. Ismay believed that Ken needed hospitalization. He changed the prescription to stronger antidepressants. Later that day Dr. Ismay called and told Ken that a psychiatrist would call at Ken's apartment the next morning. Ken said that he was feeling better on the new antidepressants, and so Dr. Ismay changed the appointment to August 10.

The end came between 2 am and 4 am on August 9, 1967. Ken beat Joe to death with a hammer. The blows caved in Joe's skull, and brain was spattered on the walls and the ceiling. Ken was covered with blood, and he took off his pajamas. He then took twenty-two Nembutals and died.

Ken's life was in many ways the life of a typical suicide. He lost his mother in a particularly traumatic way when he was eleven. His father then killed himself when Ken was twenty three. These experiences are very common in individuals who later commit suicide.

In his career, Ken was a failure. He was a bad actor and did not graduate from RADA. He could not get his writing published or sell his paintings. For most of his adult life, Ken was sustained by his close relationship with Joe. Although Joe was incredibly promiscuous, always on the lookout for a casual sexual encounter, these other sexual experiences were casual. Ken remained his only lover.

However, as Joe's success grew, Ken was faced with the contrast between Joe's fame and his own failure. Sensitized by the earlier loss of his mother (and his father), Ken could not face losing Joe. The murder-suicide served to escape from the unbearable pain of his life and to destroy the person he had come to hate.

Joe was a successful comic playwright, but as a human being he seems to have been thoroughly obnoxious. He was alienated from his family. He had few friends, though many acquaintances. He was involved in a long-term relationship with Ken, but continually cruised through the public toilets of London and the beaches of Morocco for casual sex. He was involved, admittedly, with a very neurotic individual in Ken, but Joe does not seem to have had the interpersonal skills to build a good relationship.

Joe was a self-centered, angry and vulgar person. But what is of interest here is the possibility that he played a role in precipitating his own murder. Was Joe committing suicide by getting someone to kill him?

Ken had threatened suicide many times to Joe, and so Joe knew that Ken was in a state of despair. Joe had refused to have sex with Ken for years, and Joe's sexual indifference to Ken was contrasted by his strong sexual appetite for strangers. Not only this, but Joe documented all of this in his diary which he knew Ken read. In the last few weeks of their life, Ken had in fact physically attacked Joe.

In this situation, it would be reasonable to fear for your life. You would take care not to antagonize the other person, and you would try to get out of the situation quickly and carefully. Not Joe.

To some extent, therefore, it seems reasonable to conclude that Joe played a role in precipitating his own murder and that this may have been motivated in part by his own, possibly unconscious, suicidal motives.

17. MARK ROTHKO:

MODERN AMERICAN PAINTER

Mark Rothko was born as Marcus Rothkovich on September 25, 1903, in the city of Dvinsk in what would later be called Latvia. His father, Jacob was a wealthy pharmacist. Marcus had a sister Sonya fourteen years older, a brother Moise eleven years older and a brother Albert eight years older.

After Mark's birth, his father became more religious, and, whereas the older children had gone to the public schools, Marcus was sent to the Jewish school. Dvinsk was spared the pogroms against the Jews in Russia, but the fear of persecution led the family to plan emigrating to America. Jacob arrived at Ellis Island in 1910 and went to Oregon to join his brother there. His two older sons escaped to America through the underground (to avoid serving in the Czar's army), and in 1913 Jacob sent the money for his wife and Mark to come. They settled in Portland, Oregon, as the Rothkowitzs, but Jacob died after seven months.

Mark finished high school by the time he was seventeen and developed an early reputation as a radical. In 1921, Mark set off for Yale University on a full scholarship. Mark studied hard and worked, first as a waiter and then in a laundry, to meet expenses. However, after six months, Yale took away his scholarship. (In those days Yale University, like many other universities, discriminated against Jews.) Mark was told that he must borrow the money from Yale if he wanted to attend, and Yale dunned Mark for many years for the money he owed.

After two years, Mark quit. He moved to New York City and took various jobs to get by. He happened to find himself at a drawing class one day when he went to meet a friend there, and he was intrigued. In January 1924, he joined the Art Students League, and he sampled classes there for the next two years.

During the late 1920s, Mark illustrated maps for books, but he had to sue the publisher for the royalties he had been promised. He lost in court. In 1929, Mark taught part-time at the Center Academy in Brooklyn, and he continued to teach on and off for the next thirty years to supplement his income from painting, although he disliked teaching.

At the Catskills for a holiday he met Edith Sacher, also from Brooklyn. They fell in love and married, but it was a mismatch. Mark was a melancholic romantic Russian with a desire to be a painter. Edith was pragmatic and worked as a jewelry designer.

The Depression brought rewards, for Roosevelt's programs included the Federal Art Project. Mark had exhibitions of his work in Portland and New York in 1933, and in 1935 he was hired by the Project. One result of the Project was to bring artists together, and Mark was part of a group of dissidents who attacked the establishment. They got attention but sold few paintings. Mark became a citizen in 1938 and in the 1940s changed his name to Marcus Rothko. (He later changed it to Mark Rothko.)

Mark's first works were representational paintings of city scenes and surrealistic seascapes in watercolor. This early work sold poorly and was barely noticed by the major art critics. During the Second World War, he and Edith divorced, and in 1944 he met Mary Alice Beistle (known as Mell), an illustrator of children's books, Protestant and from Cleveland. They married in 1945.

After the war, the artist's community in New York City remained tightly knit, with Mark belonging to the uptown group. Their life was consumed by producing and discussing art works. In 1946, Mark had surrealistic seascapes on show in San Francisco and Santa Barbara.

He also taught at the California School of Fine Arts for two summers.

In 1947, he began to explore new directions for his paintings and produced misty forms of color suspended in space. Eventually, his style of paintings, along with the works of other contemporaries, became known as the New York School of Abstract Expressionism. They opened a school of art and published periodicals. Mark sold his pictures to the Whitney Museum and to museums in San Francisco and Brooklyn. However, his total income from painting and teaching in 1949 was $3935, leaving him $1387 after paying for materials. To support the family, Mark gave up part-time teaching and joined the faculty full-time at Brooklyn College.

Still angry at the Whitney Museum for their lack of support of contemporary artists in the past, Mark refused to have his works exhibited there (though he had sold them some paintings), but he was included in a show at the Museum of Modern Art. He also refused to let his works be shown abroad where he would have no control over how they were hung. After Brooklyn College denied him tenure, Mark was thrown into reliance on sales of his paintings.

In the late 1950s, art collecting took off. Millionaires discovered art both as an investment and as a tax shelter. Dealers proliferated, and prices soared. Works by Mark (as well as Willem de Kooning and Jackson Pollock) were mentioned by Fortune as good investments.

But at this time too, just when poverty was ending for Mark, his psychological state began to deteriorate. He had always been an insomniac and moody. But now his melancholic moods turned into depressions, and his moods swung from one extreme to another. His friends described him as a volcano. He was worried about money even though he had enough. On one occasion, the theft of his bank statements led to a bout of depression.

His drinking increased, and he became a hypochondriac but with a distrust of doctors. In 1956, he developed a fever and painful swollen joints. After three months in bed, he allowed a doctor to see him (but not take a blood sample). He had gout. When he finally permitted treatment, his doctor also discovered hypertension. But Mark refused to have regular medical checkups.

As his fame as a painter grew, Mark became increasingly concerned about what was written about him. He disliked being identified with the New York School. He disliked the comments made about his work by critics. He began to worry intensely about how his work should best be exhibited, both during his life and after his death.

However, his years of poverty were over. Mark and Mell bought a little cottage in Provincetown and were eventually able to move into better apartments and better studios. Bernard Reis became his financial advisor, and Mark's worries now focussed on taxes and how to avoid them. Mark was very frustrated over the structure of the art profession. Universities, museums and the art dealers all frustrated and angered him. Although some of his anger seemed excessive, abuses were widespread. Favoritism was common, art dealers wrote contracts that exploited the artists, and financial advisers mismanaged their clients.

Despite these abuses, Mark's income increased dramatically during the 1960s. He bought a house for $75,000 on East Fifty-Ninth Street. He found a good studio (in the East Sixties), and he sold paintings both through dealers (eventually working with Frank Lloyd and Marlborough Galleries) and independently. In 1961, he was invited to the Kennedy inaugural. His paintings were fetching $20,000. And he had a retrospective at the Museum of Modern Art: fifty seven paintings.

In 1962, Mark became acutely depressed. His brother Albert had cancer, and the art world was turning to "Pop" art as the new fad. In late 1962, at the age of fifty-nine (Mell was forty-one), he had a son, Christopher.

In 1964, John and Dominique de Menil commissioned Mark to paint murals for a new chapel in Houston. This project occupied him for the next few years. When he finished in 1966, he had painted fourteen murals and eight experimental studies. The project dominated his life and drained him emotionally and physically. Visitors to his studio described him as pompous, self-centered, and hostile. He banished friends who failed to praise him sufficiently. One visitor recalls being criticized by Mark for conversing with him rather than immediately going to view the new paintings.

Mark continued to be successful financially. He limited sales of his paintings to keep their prices high, and for those he sold personally he demanded cash. In 1968, his murals for the Houston Chapel were ready, and the Tate Gallery in London had purchased an earlier set of murals he had painted. But then one day he felt a pain in his back, and his legs went numb. He had suffered an aneurysm of the aorta, brought on by arteriosclerosis and hypertension. He stayed in the hospital for three weeks, and, although he recovered physically, he remained distressed by this illness.

His depression intensified, and his health became an obsession. His egotism turned into self-pity, guilt and doubt. The mistrust he had for the art world became paranoid. His alcohol abuse worsened. His anger began to focus more on Mell, and the marriage deteriorated. (Although he loved flirting with other women, he probably had only three serious affairs during his marriage. Unfortunately, one of his lovers told Mell about her affair with Mark. Thus, the marriage had seen problems all along.) Mell was tiring of tending to this self-centered, drunken genius, and she too turned to alcohol. Mark began to consider separation.

He also began to plan for the Mark Rothko Foundation, the focus of which was primarily to preserve his work and to arrange for its display after his death. Mark wanted to ensure his fame and prominence, and the foundation was the center of his plan for immortality in the art world. The foundation would keep the works together and arrange exhibits in proper groupings in suitable lighting. However, this work on the Foundation also depressed him since it brought home the imminence of his death.

As his drinking (and cigarette smoking) increased, his depression worsened. Bernard Reis took him to see Dr. Nathan Kline who specialized in tranquilizers and antidepressants. Kline gave him Valium and a new antidepressant in addition to the pills Mark was taking for hypertension, gout and insomnia.

By the end of 1968, Mark had a rebellious teenage daughter (Kate was seventeen), a rambunctious five-year old and an unhappy, alcoholic wife. Mark moved out on New Year's Day, 1969, to his studio. He still supported the family financially, returned for laundry and occasional meals, and checked on his family all the time. He began seeing a widow, Rita Reinhardt, who entertained hopes of marrying him, but it appears that he was impotent in the later years of his life. He feared being finished (impotent) as an artist. Although he was now a millionaire, he lived frugally, like a pauper.

However, he did begin painting again, a series of paintings of blacks on grays that many visitors saw as signs of impending doom. He became more dependent on his friends, desperately seeking their approval of his paintings, fearing abandonment. He needed people for lunch and to talk to at odd hours. Friends were forced to disconnect their telephones at night to avoid being awakened. At meals with the family, there would be fights over Rita and over the food Mell served him. His daughter found him usually depressed and uncommunicative.

Still successes continued. In June, 1969, there was a Rothko room at an exhibition at the Museum of Modern Art. The price for his paintings reached over $50,000. In October, 1969, the Metropolitan Museum had a show of modern artists including ten of Mark's paintings, but the show angered Mark and exacerbated his self-doubt and fears for his stature in the art world.

During the summer of 1969, his mood worsened. During a visit to a doctor (Alan Mead) he was totally disoriented, disturbed and dazed. Mead cut his dosage of Valium and Mellaril, sent a report of this to Kline, and tried to persuade Mark to see a psychotherapist, but Mark refused. His drunkenness worsened, even to the point of losing control of his bodily functions.

By November, Mark was desperate. He called his regular physician (Dr. Albert Grokest). Kline had given him new pills. Grokest was upset by this treatment that was independent of his own and told Mark not to take Kline's medication. Kline requested a meeting with Grokest, but Grokest refused to meet with him.

On January 27, 1970, Mark visited Mead because Grokest had gone to Mexico. He was taking large amounts of Valium. He was unable to work and felt pressured by his family and by Rita. He was impotent. He could sleep only with the use of chloral hydrate. He had gout, emphysema from chain-smoking and a hernia. He was worried about his hypertension, but his blood pressure was normal. By February, his worsening eyesight added an extra stress. He seemed to be painting again and demanding that friends visit him. They noticed that his memory was deteriorating.

He had agreed to let the Marlborough Gallery enter his storehouse on Wednesday February 25 to select paintings to purchase, although he had never before allowed people into his storehouse. Mark had always made the selections himself. On Thursday February 19 he dined and fought with his family. Over the weekend, he seemed withdrawn and was seen sitting alone in Central Park.

On Tuesday he kept his appointment with Dr. Mead. His condition seemed a little better, but he was still agitated and depressed. He had an appointment with Kline on Friday. On Tuesday night he dined with Rita. She thought he was full of rage and frustration over the selecting of his paintings the next day. Rita reassured him that he could refuse to let the gallery representatives see his storehouse.

At 9 am on Wednesday, Mark's assistant let himself into the studio. In the kitchen, he saw Mark stretched out on the floor. He had slashed his arms in the crooks of the elbows. It was suspected that he had taken barbiturates too.

Mark's psychological state clearly worsened in the last few years of his life, and he refused psychotherapy to supplement the medications he was given. However, what is noteworthy in Mark's case is the conflict between the various physicians involved in the treatment of Mark. The physicians seemed more focused on their mutual rivalry than in deciding what was best for their patient, Mark. In competing with one another rather than collaborating, they increased the likelihood that Mark would kill himself.

18. JAMES FORRESTAL:

SECRETARY OF DEFENSE

James Forrestal is the highest ranking government official in America to have committed suicide. So far. In the early hours of Sunday May 22, 1949, Forrestal tied one end of his dressing gown sash to a radiator and the other end around his neck. He then jumped from the window of a kitchen on the sixteenth floor of a building at the Bethesda Naval Hospital where he had been hospitalized for psychiatric reasons. The sash broke, and Forrestal fell to his death on the roof of a third floor passageway.

Forrestal was no longer an official of the government. He had resigned from his position as Secretary of Defense and left office on March 28. But his personal problems had begun much earlier, and so it is clear that he was mentally disturbed while in office. This raises the fascinating problem of what would happen if such an affliction ever occurred in the President of the nation. The stuff that novels are made of.

James was born in the small town of Matteawan, New York, about sixty miles from New York City, on February 15, 1892. He was the third child of James and Mary Forrestal. His mother's father, Mathias Toohey, had settled in Matteawan in the 1840s and soon owned a large farm. The first Catholic service in the town was held at his home. His daughter Mary became a school teacher. Forrestal's father, James, arrived in 1857 from Ireland at the age of nine to join his mother (who was in service with a family) and his step father. He became an apprentice carpenter, and in 1857 he organized his own construction company. He became a Major in the National Guard and was active in Democratic party politics.

The force in the home was Mary Forrestal. She was a strict disciplinarian and closely supervised the education of her three sons. If they misbehaved, she punished them with a strap or by sending them to bed without supper. She was a staunch Catholic and insisted that the family attend Mass regularly. She did not tolerate swearing, jokes or pulp magazines. Her hobby was music.

James was sickly as a child and, in addition to the usual childhood diseases, had pneumonia. He looked frail, and later in life he made an effort to build himself up physically through sports and exercise. At the age of twenty five he was five feet nine and a half and weighed one hundred and fifty pounds.

He started in a parochial school but moved on to the public high school. He graduated in June 1908 at the age of sixteen and then worked as a journalist for three years. In 1911 he entered Dartmouth University, but transferred after a year to Princeton University. Six weeks before graduation, he withdrew and so never received his degree. He refused to attend the lectures in one course and, when threatened with failure, decided to withdraw rather than retake the course in the following year. His parents had wanted him to be a priest and so were disappointed by his choices. It was as if Mother had son Will, Father had son Henry, and so God could have son James.

James had transferred to Princeton because he had aspirations and thought that Princeton would advance his career more than Dartmouth. In his senior year, he was editor of the Daily Princetonian and was voted by his class as the man most likely to succeed.

Although his family gave him financial support, James was continually in financial distress. His friends at Princeton did not know of his family's contributions and believed him to be from a poor home. James did not want to accept money from his family and felt guilty about it when he did.

There was little love or affection from James's parents which probably made it hard for him to establish close and warm relationships with others. The home was restrictive, and James came to reject the Catholic and parochial attitudes of his family. He became estranged from his family and in later life was moody, taciturn and withdrawn. When at Princeton, he rarely visited his home. Although he wrote to his parents and brothers, he did not confide in them. He rarely discussed his family with friends, and many did not know where he came from. His two sons did not meet their Matteawan relatives until after their father died.

His parents, and particularly his mother, never forgave him for rejecting the priesthood and the Church, and he suffered from guilt too. In 1925 he rented an apartment in New York City for his mother and bought her a fur coat. But she accepted neither gift and died in October that year.

He had three brief jobs before beginning to work for Dillon Read as a bond salesman in 1916. By 1919 he was head of the sales department in New York City (despite a break during the First World War for training as a naval aviator), by 1923 a partner, by 1926 a vice-president, and in 1938 at the age of forty six he became its president.

The 1920s saw him sharing an apartment with three other bachelors. He was ambitious, driven and dedicated. He had little social life, working long hours. He dressed expensively, went to concerts, and lived well.

He chose Josephine Ogden to be his wife, divorced and an editor at Vogue. They were married in October 1926. A Thursday. His colleagues at Dillon Read had no warning of the marriage, and James was back at work on Monday. James believed that husbands and wives were entitled to lead separate lives, and he did not want children. In a few years he had constructed such a marriage. The sociable, gay and witty Josephine could not get on with the workaholic James. As the years passed, they spent less and less time with each other, and they were cold and distant to each other. At the time of her husband's hospitalization, just ten days prior to his suicide, Josephine left for Paris.

But they did have children. Michael born in 1927 and Peter born in 1930. The two sons saw little of their father during their childhood and adolescence. He sent them to boarding schools in America and abroad, and the two children were raised primarily by the servants. James was often away and, when he was at home, he would send for them on Friday evenings to find out about their week, meetings that were nerve-wracking for James and for them. He was stingy with them and believed in forcing their independence, even in crises. James not only kept physically distant from them, but he showed them no affection. Only in later life did he show any interest in their lives.

Thus, James had a cold relationship with a wife and a cold relationship with his sons. James did not seem to know how to relate closely or warmly to his family, or perhaps he did not want to. He lacked either the necessary social skills or the motivation.

Was he schizoid? It is hard to say. None of those who remember him describe him as being hard to understand, suspicious or manifesting any psychiatric symptoms. And his success both in his Wall Street career and later in politics make it unlikely that he was psychotic or pre-psychotic at this time. Eccentric perhaps.

To give one example of his success at Dillon Read, it was James who arranged for his company to purchase Dodge and later sell it to Chrysler at a profit. In 1933, he was investigated by a Senate committee for his financial dealings (in which he had netted nearly a million dollars profit for himself and avoided paying taxes), but in those days there was no regulating agency (such as the Securities and Exchange Commission), and he was never found to have behaved unlawfully.

He was soon invited to join the government. From 1940 to 1944, James was Under-Secretary of the Navy, from 1944 to 1947 Secretary of the Navy, and from 1947 to 1949 the first Secretary of Defense. His government career started off well. The country would soon be at war and, as Under-Secretary, James gathered a competent staff and began to reform the methods by which the Navy ordered and purchased material. However, as he worked longer and longer in the government, James seemed to antagonize more and more people, perhaps inevitable for a bureaucrat who wants to change things.

As Under-Secretary, he had disagreements with the Fleet Commander-in-Chief, Ernest King, who never forgave James for fighting his reorganization plans that would have given the Fleet Commander increased power over the civilians (that is, the Secretary and the Under-Secretary of the Navy). King lost that fight.

James always had trouble dealing with authority figures. (James would have problems later with President Truman too.) But there is no hint of this problem in James's business career. Perhaps in business, success in your financial deals is required rather than the negotiation and compromises necessary for bureaucratic success.

As James moved upwards in his government career, he developed a distrust of the communists and of the Russians, and he worked long and hard to convince others of this. He also encouraged attempts to root out communist infiltration in the labor movement, academia, the government and the media. James wanted the United States to be militarily ready for any eventuality. James's office became the clearinghouse for information related to the communist influence in the world.

James was competent. It was his reorganization of the Navy Department that facilitated the production of the ships and material that led to the victories at Midway and Guadalcanal in the War. When the Secretary of the Navy died in office in 1944, Roosevelt had no hesitation in nominating James for the position.

However, as Secretary of the Navy, James soon had to deal with the new President, Truman, for whom he had less respect and with whom he agreed less than he had with Roosevelt. He also had to deal with peacetime rather than war. His opinions brought him into increasing conflict with Truman. On the one hand, as a member of the cabinet, he was supposed to support Truman. On the other hand, in speeches and in front of congressional committees, he was asked for his opinion, and his opinion was usually more hawkish and more anti-communist than Truman's. In particular, he took an anti-Zionist position because he saw the oil in the Middle East as vital for the United States and he felt that we should not antagonize the Arabs. This led to James being seen as anti-semitic as well as anti-Zionist.

As James became increasingly at odds with other members of the administration and government, he began to become suspicious of the motivations of those opposed to his positions. At the same time, more and more people began to attack James for his positions. These attacks had begun even while he was Under-Secretary. For example, in 1940 he, along with others, was accused by the press of wanting to establish a complete military dictatorship.

During James's years in office, the Russians indeed fulfilled his expectations. In May 1947, a communist government took over in Hungary, and in February 1948 the Czechoslovakian President appointed a pro-Soviet cabinet.

The decision to unify the services under a Secretary of Defense also led to a great deal of fighting over different proposals. Although he was initially opposed to this, James eventually saw it as inevitable and sought to shape the new office. He did not approve of the proposal being considered by Truman, and his lobbying against it bordered on insubordination. He expected to be asked to resign as Secretary because of his strong opposition, but the request for his resignation was never made. He was accused of stifling dissent in the Navy, the unit of which he was the civilian head.

However, when the new department was created, James was nominated to be the first Secretary of Defense, although he was not the first choice for the position. There was criticism of his appointment from liberal groups, but most of the media praised the decision. When he accepted the position, James said that this would be his last position and that he might only stay another year. Most of his friends ignored these protestations and assumed that James eventually wanted to become President. He had already been asked whether he would run for Governor of New York and whether he would stand as a candidate for Vice-President.

During 1948, James's relationship with Truman deteriorated badly for they differed on many political issues. In the election of 1948, James was thought by Democrats to be supporting Dewey rather than Truman, and he made it clear that he would like to serve as Secretary of Defense or State under Dewey. After Truman's victory, James submitted his resignation which is traditional upon the election of a President, and he expected it to be accepted. Surprisingly, Truman wanted him to continue, and James consented to do so.

In contrast to his success as Under-Secretary of the Navy, James felt that he had failed in his attempts to unify the services as Secretary of Defense. He was also exhausted, both physically and mentally. Some of his friends urged him to resign, but he would not.

By 1948, James was losing weight and had little appetite. He had digestive disturbances, insomnia and chronic fatigue. His aides noticed nervous habits, such as dipping his fingers in his water glass and moistening his lips. He picked at one part of his scalp which, therefore, became quite sore. He began to postpone decisions and to worry about those already made. He would revise and re-revise speeches. He had memory slips and made mistakes in identity. (At home, James once asked the butler where the butler was.)

Truman found out about this and ordered the Secret Service to investigate. They discovered that James had acquired a large quantity of sleeping pills and had made out a will. James was also showing great suspiciousness. He was worried who might be at the door whenever the bell rang. He suspected that the communists and the Jews were out to get him fired and that Stuart Symington, the Secretary for the Air force with whom he had serious disagreements, was spying on him. The Secret Service concluded that James was suffering from a psychosis with suicidal features. But most of his colleagues and friends did not realize the severity of the breakdown and put James's behavior down to fatigue.

There is some disagreement about James's resignation. James was probably told in January that Louis Johnson would succeed him on or about May 1. On March 1, Truman summoned James and asked for a letter of resignation. James seemed to be stunned by the suddenness of this request. James slept little that night and arrived at the office the next morning haggard, depressed and exhausted. He finally composed a satisfactory letter and resigned as of March 31. He was vague when asked by reporters about his future plans. He denied that he was to be President of Princeton University or that he planned to write a book. The press did report that James and his wife planned to travel to England, and reservations were made on the Queen Mary.

James was present on March 28 when his successor was sworn in. On March 29 James received various honors and plaudits from members of the government. Later that day an aide found him in his office, sitting rigid, with his hat on. He seemed to be unaware that anyone had entered the room. He was bewildered to find he no longer had a limousine at his disposal. His aide arranged to get him driven home and called a friend, Ferdinand Eberstadt, to come over and stay with James. Eberstadt found James agitated and depressed. James told Eberstadt that he was a complete failure and was considering suicide. He blamed his firing on the Jews and communists. He suspected that they were in the house right then, and he even searched the house for them.

Eberstadt called the new Secretary of Defense who arranged to have James flown to Florida to stay with his wife and friends. An Air Force plane flew him down that evening. His first words as he stepped off the plane were, "Bob, they're after me."

During the next few days, James made at least one suicide attempt, and as a result all knives, razor blades, and belts were hidden. His family made sure that James was accompanied at all times, whether shaving, swimming or simply out walking. James told one friend that the metal holders for beach umbrellas were wired and that everything said was being recorded. He believed that the communists were about to invade the United States and at times talked as if the invasion had already occurred. He believed that he was targeted for assassination.

He also recognized that he needed psychiatric help. Dr. William Menninger flew in on March 30 to talk to James, and Dr. George Raines, chief psychiatrist at the

Bethesda Naval Hospital, flew in the next day. Menninger concluded that James had a severe depression seen usually in soldiers with operational fatigue. It was decided to hospitalize James, and he was flown to the Bethesda Naval Hospital on April 2.

James was sedated for the flight, but he was nonetheless very agitated. He talked of suicide and his enemies. He wondered whether he was being punished for being a bad Catholic and for marrying a divorced woman. On the way from Washington airport to the hospital, he tried to leave the car, but was restrained. He said that he did not expect to leave the hospital alive, but it is not clear whether he was referring to suicide or to assassination.

Raines diagnosed James as having involutional melancholia, a form of psychotic depression in middle-aged people. James spent seven weeks at the hospital. He was given narcosis during the first week, followed by insulin therapy and daily psychotherapy. Raines noted that the depression got worse toward the end of each week.

James showed some improvement. He gained weight, and his depression seemed less severe. At the beginning of May, James was given more freedom. He was allowed to visit other patients on the floor and to use the kitchen. His brother visited, as did President Truman and Secretary of Defense Johnson.

Raines stopped the daily psychotherapy on May 14 and left for a professional association meeting in Montreal on May 18. James's wife left for Europe on May 12 and his son Michael for Europe on May 13. (His son Peter was working in Washington.)

On Friday May 20 James seemed fine despite the fact it was the end of the week. On the evening of Saturday May 21 James declined a sedative and sleeping pill. At 1.45 am on Sunday May 22, he was observed to be copying a poem by Sophocles. Shortly afterwards, he jumped from the window of the kitchen.

During his government career, James had realistically been concerned about the intentions of Russia and communists toward the free world. He suspected them of imperial desires and he was, on the whole, correct. In his psychotic delusions, this rational fear was translated into a fear of personal persecution by his enemies, both anonymous (Jews and communists in general) and known opponents (such as Stuart Symington).

Those who admired and agreed with James's views saw his suicide as brought about by the hostile journalists who had attacked him, especially in the few years prior to his death (including Drew Pearson and Walter Winchell). James really was attacked in the public media and in this sense had real enemies. James was hurt by these attacks, which were not only on his political beliefs but also on his personal honor, integrity and courage. Even paranoids can have real enemies. Certainly, these attacks may have nourished his delusions of persecution.

Our problem is that we see only hints of this eventual disintegration in his youth: lack of warmth from his parents, their rejection of him and hostility toward his career choice, and his estrangement from his family; a strange relationship with his wife and with his sons. But nothing in the reports of those who knew James back then suggests psychosis or even a personality disorder that might develop into a psychosis.

James was a loner, an isolated man, with success on Wall Street and initial success in government, who eventually ran into people who disagreed with his world view and under whose opposition he seemed to break down. He lacked the self-confidence to withstand opposition and hostility, and he had never developed the social relationships, especially with a wife, that would help him survive rough times. A colleague recalls him calling one Christmas Day to suggest a game of golf, as if he did not know that people spent Christmas with their families. It is interesting to speculate on what might have happened if James had stayed on Wall Street. There were no signs of deterioration during his career there. Would that environment, one in which he had been very successful, have protected him from disintegration? Or was his psychosis quietly developing, getting ready to bloom when he reached middle age?

19. JUDY GARLAND:

SELF-DESTRUCTIVE MOVIE STAR

Judy Garland rose to become a famous movie star and singer. For all of her adult life, she was addicted to drugs, and she made numerous suicide attempts. Judy died from an overdose of sleeping pills in London on June 22, 1969. Her daughter, Liza Minelli, and her biographer both believe that Judy's death was accidental, but this seems unlikely. We will see that Judy was very likely to kill herself and that in all probability she did.

Frank Gumm came from Tennessee and his wife Ethel from Michigan. They worked together entertaining movie audiences. After their first two daughters were born, Mary Jane (Suzy) on September 24, 1915, and Virginia (Jimmy) on July 4, 1917, Frank decided to settle down, and he leased the movie theater in Grand Rapids, Minnesota, supplementing his earnings with a job on the local newspaper. Ethel, helped him, selling tickets and playing the piano during the silent movies. Her daughters sang for the audience during the intermission.

When Ethel got pregnant again, she and Frank decided to have an abortion, but a friend persuaded them that it was too dangerous. They hoped for a son, but Judy was born two weeks overdue on June 10, 1922, named Frances Gumm. Judy grew up knowing this — that she was unwanted, that her parents wanted a son and that she was overdue.

When she was two-and-a-half, Judy made her stage debut at her father's movie theater, and soon the parents had created an act for the three Gumm sisters. In June 1926, the parents moved to Los Angeles. Frank leased a movie theater in Lancaster, north of Los Angeles on the edge of the Mojave Desert.

Ethel devoted much attention to her daughters' careers. She enrolled them in the local dance school, she gave them music lessons, and she had them sing. In late 1927, she enrolled them in a dance school in Los Angeles which had been a springboard for many stars. Judy enjoyed this, but she also missed the fun of childhood and disliked the early hours and continual lessons. Eventually Suzy and Jimmy dropped out of the weekend lessons in Los Angeles. Ethel was the typical pushy stage-mother and took Judy for auditions. Judy, however, began to enjoy the enthusiastic response of an audience. The Gumm sisters still performed as an act together, and word began to spread about the child with the incredible voice. Judy next enrolled in Los Angeles in a school for professional children. Several people worked on getting Judy, as she was now called, a movie contract. She sang for Joe Mankiewicz, she sang for Ida Koverman who worked for Louis B. Mayer (the head of Metro-Goldwyn-Mayer), and soon she sang for Mayer himself, who signed her without a screen test in September, 1935, when she was thirteen.

Metro continued the special treatment that Judy had always experienced. Metro's Special Services Department was one of the most extraordinary finishing schools in the world. It provided her education, even building a small classroom near the set when she was working on a movie. She had a voice coach, was given dance lessons, speech lessons, drama lessons, make-up lessons, and deportment lessons, and had a physical therapist and specialists to help her lose weight.

Metro was a factory, designed to turn out fifty-two movies a year to send to their theater chain (Loew's). Three thousand people worked in Culver City making this possible. But, of course, this led to intense scrutiny and competition between the actors. Judy was short and plump, with scoliosis (a slight curvature of the spine which ran in her mother's family). Her teeth were crooked and her nose a problem. (Judy had to wear removable caps on her teeth and rubber discs in her nose when on screen.) She also had to continually fight excessive weight above her waist. Judy was humiliated by all of these judgments and by comparison with her peers. Judy soon came to believe that she was not physically attractive or sexually desirable to men, and certainly inferior to the other teenagers there (who included Lana Turner, Elizabeth Taylor and Hedy Lamarr). Ethel would remind Judy that she was signed for her voice, but that was not enough for Judy.

Judy's voice coach, Roger Edens, worked with her intensively to develop her ability as a singer, and Ethel came to the studio every day to rehearse and accompany her. But seven weeks after she signed with Metro, her father died without warning (of a massive hemorrhage of the mastoid). Judy took the pillow her father had lain on and slept on it for many nights, resisting all efforts to wash it. His death was a profound shock for her, and she spent much of her life looking for a father figure to replace him. Most of her close friends were males, and she was truly happy only when she was in love.

Her first two roles were in a short movie Every Sunday with Metro and a small part in Pigskin Parade for Twentieth Century Fox. Her first major movie role was in Broadway Melody of 1938 and, for this movie, the studio began giving Judy Benzedrine and phenobarbital to help her lose weight and to sleep at nights. These were the new wonder drugs for the movie colony in California, and no one was aware of their addictive potential. For Judy, their use for Broadway Melody began her life-long dependence on drugs.

Broadway Melody was released in the Fall of 1937, and the reviews of Judy's performance were enthusiastic. After several more movies, usually with Judy cast as the girl who never gets the man she loves,

MGM decided to build a movie especially for Judy, The Wizard of Oz. The movie was released in August, 1939, and Judy went on a publicity tour with Mickey Rooney. Before one performance, Judy collapsed backstage and could not go on, the first of many such collapses in her life as a performer.

In November, Ethel eloped with Will Gilmore, her long-time lover now recently widowed, to Arizona where she married him on the fourth anniversary of Frank Gumm's death. Judy never forgave her mother for this.

Although Judy had several crushes, her first love was Artie Shaw, in his late twenties and twice divorced. She confided to him her self-doubts. She saw herself as homely, fat and ugly. She was aware that the vibrato in her voice could get out of control. Artie was never aware that Judy was in love with him. He never thought of Judy as someone to love or make love to. In February 1940, Judy read in the newspapers that Artie had eloped with Lana Turner (who was one of Judy's rivals at Metro). Judy had seen him three nights before his elopement and had no idea that he was in love with anyone else. Although they remained friends, she felt that he had forsaken her, just as her father had five years earlier by his death.

Judy's adolescence was drawing to a close. In the Spring of 1940 she received a special Oscar for the best juvenile performance (in The Wizard of Oz). Later that year, Louis Mayer gave her an eighteenth birthday party at his house, and raised her salary from $750 to $3000 a week. She fell in love with David Rose, the leader of an orchestra, and married him in July, 1941, after fights with her mother about her affair with him. It was Judy who pushed for the marriage. She loved him, but she also wanted to get away from her mother's control.

And thus begins the end.

It seems strange to see Judy's life at age nineteen as beginning its decline. Although she was a major star already, many of her famous performances were still ahead of her. But her life from now on was simply a repetition. The same events, catastrophes, and breakdowns keep reoccurring again and again, except with increasing seriousness. Let us look at the major themes.

Her Mother
Ethel had shaped Judy's life and continued to try to maintain control. She was opposed to most of Judy's loves and lovers. Ethel's marriage to Will increased the alienation Judy felt, though that marriage lasted less than four years. After a serious row with Judy in 1949, Ethel moved to Dallas to live near her daughter Jimmy. She moved back to Los Angeles eventually to try to help Judy, but Judy refused to see her. She left word with servants not to admit Ethel, even to see the grandchildren. Ethel died in January 1953, in Los Angeles after a heart attack in the parking lot of the factory where she worked for $61 a week. Judy did go to the funeral.

Marriages
Her marriage with David Rose was soon over. Their careers kept them busy and apart. They had different life styles, and Judy's dependence on the drugs was a problem. They separated in the Spring of 1943 and divorced in 1944.

She next married Vincente Minelli in 1945. Vincente made her feel that she was an attractive women, and he admired her talent as an actress. Liza was born in March 1946, and Judy had problems coping with a husband, a house, a child and a career, especially while addicted to drugs. The marriage deteriorated, and Judy moved out in December 1950. The divorce was final in March 1952.

She married Sidney Luft in June 1952, already pregnant with Lorna who was born in November 1952. (Joey was born in 1955, at which time Judy had her tubes tied.) Sid devoted himself to Judy, and he abandoned his own career in order to manage Judy's. But marital conflicts grew over the years, and they separated in 1958 and began a seven year period of fights, reconciliations and separations. Finally, they were divorced in 1965, whereupon Judy married Mark Herron a younger man. This marriage lasted only six months before they separated. There was then a succession of affairs until she married another younger man, Mickey Deans, in January 1969. Five months later Judy was dead.

Judy's Career

By the time she was twenty-two, Judy had been in nineteen films. For 1943 through 1945 she was voted one of the five most popular screen actresses. However, Judy's drug and emotional problems began to interfere with her work. She was usually late to work, if she arrived, and temperamental to work with. MGM paid a psychiatrist to be with her on the set in 1947. MGM had to suspend her frequently and fired her from three movies (including Annie Get Your Gun). In September 1950, MGM cancelled her contract, almost fifteen years to the day after they signed her.

Judy had little or no ability to handle her financial affairs. Her mother and financial advisers had tried to plan wisely but failed. After her divorce from Minelli and her firing from MGM, Judy was continually in debt. In 1950, she and Minelli owed $60,000 in back taxes and thousands more to friends. (In 1966, Judy's assets were listed as $12,000 and her liabilities to 120 creditors were $122,000.)

In 1950, Judy was free from contractual obligations.

She could do radio, concerts and films at will. During most of this period she was married to Sidney Luft, and he often acted as a business manager for her. Her freedom was, however, superficial. She was in debt so often that she had to work in order to pay her bills. However, her drug addiction and increasing psychological disturbance led her to cancel performances and walk out on contracts, so that often she could not even cover the expenses of the tour she had embarked on.

She appeared in A Star Is Born in 1954, Judgment At Nuremberg in 1961, A Child Is Waiting in 1962, followed by I Could Go On Singing. She continued to give concerts, some outstanding and others where she was booed off the stage (as in Australia in 1964), collapsed on stage, or simply went to sleep in the middle of a song.

Drugs And Breakdowns

Judy was addicted to uppers and downers, amphetamines and barbiturates. Severe addiction to amphetamines leads to paranoid symptoms, and Judy developed increasingly severe paranoia. (In her separations from Sid Luft, she was often convinced that he was going to kidnap her children.) In addition, she was an alcoholic. (Judy and Sid attended one meeting of Alcoholics Anonymous and one of Drugs Anonymous but did not like them.) She also smoked heavily, often while drugged, with the result that she set fire to her house on one occasion and to her hotel room on another.

She had frequent stays in hospitals and sanatoriums, mainly to dry out after a physical or psychological collapse: July 1947, March 1949 where she received six electroconvulsive shock treatments, May 1949, November 1951, and more. Eventually, her alcohol and drug abuse caused her liver to become diseased, and she was frequently hospitalized with kidney and liver problems (for example, in 1959, April 1962, and August 1963) although it is hard to be sure whether she was hospitalized for physical illnesses, to dry out from drugs, or as a result of a suicide attempt.

Judy's Mental And Physical State

Judy suffered from many symptoms, including insomnia, chronic colitis, postpartum depressions (exacerbated by having to dry out during the pregnancy), headaches, and sudden inexplicable fears (a sense of impending doom, an inability to work, and a fear that she might lose her voice). She frequently collapsed on stage (for example, at The Palace in New York in November 1951).

In 1943, she entered psychoanalysis with Ernst Simmel, but, on her own admission, continually lied to him and so probably got little benefit from it. He died in the Fall of 1947, another loss for her.

Suicidal Behavior

It had always been known that her father's Aunt Mary had killed herself by pushing her wheelchair off a bridge because she was dying from a mysterious crippling disease and did not want to be a burden to her fiancé. Judy's mother made at least one suicide attempt after a fight with Judy, taking a lethal dose of Seconal and whiskey, which necessitated her stomach being pumped.

Judy's sister Suzy (a depressed alcoholic) attempted suicide with an overdose in the Fall of 1962 and finally killed herself with an overdose in May 1964 while Judy lay recovering from an attempt at suicide with an overdose herself in Hong Kong.

Judy made numerous suicide attempts; in July 1947 after a row with Minelli, she cut her wrists while others were in the house; in June 1950 after another row with Minelli and after being fired from a movie, she tried to cut her throat; after the birth of Lorna in December 1952 she cut her throat with a razor; in the 1950s she called a friend threatening to kill herself and her son Joey; in 1957 she slashed her wrists deeply in the presence of her husband Sid; she tried to jump out of a window in front of a friend in May 1961; in July 1961 she took an overdose (or had a kidney attack); in July 1962 she took an overdose in London (and later paid a blackmailer to keep the photographs out of the press); in September 1962 she took another overdose (or had another kidney attack); in May 1964 she took a large overdose during a typhoon in Hong Kong and had her stomach pumped; in 1965 she threatened to jump out of the window in front of Mark Herron; in 1966 she slashed her face superficially after a row with Mark (and claimed he had cut her); in March 1969 she overdosed while on a concert tour in Scandinavia; and finally in June 1969 she killed herself with an overdose. Judy often seemed to have no memory of her attempts, and her biographer preferred to believe that Judy attempted suicide only under the influence of drugs.

At the time of her death she had just married Mickey Deans, a young pianist-singer who had been managing a discotheque in Manhattan. They married in London in January, 1969, and again in March in case there had been a delay in her divorce from Mark Herron. Judy was still giving concerts and went to Scandinavia in the Spring for a series. Judy and Mickey flew to New York in May, where her daughter Liza found her subdued and very thin. A physician called in by a friend tried to take her off Seconal and switch her to Thorazine. Judy and Mickey flew back to London on June 17 after Mickey's plan to open a chain of Judy Garland Theaters in America had fallen through.

At 2 am in California on the June 22, a friend called her in London (where it was 10 am) to talk to her. Mickey looked for her and found her in the bathroom, dead from an overdose.

Discussion

There is much in Judy's life of interest given her eventual suicide — a history of chronic alcohol and drug abuse, severe depressions and suicidal behavior, and problems in her marriages and relationships with friends made worse by her drug addiction. Several of these deserve discussion.

Loss

Judy experienced many losses in her life. Her father died when she was thirteen, her first love never even realized that she was in love with him and married a rival teenage star. Her mother died. Her sister killed herself. Even her psychoanalyst died. In addition, severe illnesses when she was a year old and when she was five meant separations from her mother which may have made these later losses more difficult to adjust to.

Suicidal Behavior

Her daughter Liza did not want to believe that Judy's death was suicidal, and neither did her biographer. It is clear that Judy had a chronic history of suicidal behavior, much of it nonlethal and almost always done while others were around. However, several attempts were serious, requiring stomach pumping and intensive care. She could easily have died during those attempts, and one of her wrist slashings when Sid was present was very deep. Thus, although it is clear that her suicidal behavior could be seen as impulsive, manipulative and a cry for help, this does not eliminate the possibility that Judy also, at times, truly wanted to die.

Furthermore, the timing of her final suicidal act is important. Her career and life had been disintegrating at a fast rate. She was going through lovers and husbands quite quickly, arguing with them soon after going to bed with them. She was no longer seeking father figures, but taking any new young man who was around and would bolster her self-esteem. She had been drunk and fallen asleep on stage and been booed. She was heavily in debt.

How many more friends could she find who would put up with her incredible demands? What had she to look forward to? Who would marry her next? Even her children were disengaging themselves from her. Her existence was ready for death.

The Real Judy And The Pampered Star

Judy Garland was spoiled and immature. She behaved like a child. She was incapable of caring for others or of taking care of them. These traits became more extreme as she got older, but were always there. Let me give some illustrations.

In 1963, Judy wanted her daughter Liza to be with her in California. But Liza was in her fourth month of Best Foot Forward in New York and in love with a dancer. Judy called and offered the dancer a part on her television show. When he flew to California, Liza quit her show and went to California too! When Judy wanted something, she demanded it, now and at any cost to others. (Of course, she was also jealous of Liza's growing success, as well as proud of it, and the chance of interfering with Liza's career probably played a part too, especially as her own career was in ruin.)

Judy called friends at all hours of the night to talk because she could not sleep or to summon them to her house. When she needed someone to talk at 3 am, she did not care that they had to go to work at 6 am. She fired her doctors when they balked at 2 am calls. Judy would even keep her children awake to keep her company. Lorna and Joey would be tired, but Judy would keep them awake and talk, talk, talk through the night.

In fact, Liza and Lorna had always served as therapists for Judy. They grew up to be what psychologists call "parentalized children", children who never got to experience a healthy childhood in which they can depend upon others to take care of them, but rather childhoods in which they have to take care of parents. No wonder that Judy's children eventually needed psychotherapy!

The luckiest choice she made in her lovers was Sid Luft. He devoted his life to her completely for a while. Her needs for love, attention and affection could never be satisfied, but Sid thought that he alone could do it. Even after the bitter break-up of the marriage, Judy could still turn to him, and he could not resist her entreaties.

Judy's irresponsibility in all matters worsened toward the end of her life. An example from this period epitomizes her. When in New York in 1967, Lorna, aged fourteen, was running the house, looking after her mother, picking out clothes for her and so on. One night, Judy decided to cook a meal. First she needed money. She sent friends out to borrow $200 off her ex-husband Sid. Amazingly, he gave them the money! The shopping list began with an electric meat grinder, twelve crystal goblets and twelve liqueur glasses at one of the most expensive stores in Manhattan. And then they bought the food. But Judy decided not to bother grinding the meat. She told them to call Sid and have him buy some ground meat. He did! Judy opened a can of gravy (the extent of her cooking), and they sat down to eat at 11 pm.

Of course, Judy in the 1960s was a caricature of what she had been, but she had not been too different when younger. As the young star, even before she signed with MGM, Judy saw the world as revolving around her.

But who was she? To a large extent, she was a creation first of her mother and then of the studio. She had been shaped and directed by others. Her reward was attention, praise, and eventually applause. Ethel disapproved of much of what Judy herself wanted, and so Ethel never let Judy explore her own desires but always tried to impose her own will. This was especially evident over Judy's boy friends and lovers.

By the time she broke with her mother, Judy's "real self" had been neglected to such an extent that she sought continual support for the facade she had developed. She needed admiring friends, lovers and husbands, and drugs to keep her from ever exploring herself, the Judy that saw herself as fat and ugly with a precarious voice.

Judy Garland, the star, was worth something. Frances Gumm was a frightening, dreadful and appalling prospect. Judy Garland could command others to obey her whims. Frances Gumm could not even choose clothes to wear, form healthy relationships, or earn a decent living out there in the real world.

We can see that, at the age of forty-seven, it was proving increasingly difficult for Judy to continue her life-style. She could no longer support the image that had been created. Her choice was between exploring Frances Gumm and replacing Judy Garland with a real self, or dying. She chose to die.

20. OTTO WEININGER:

AN ANTI-SEMITIC JEW

Otto's father, Leopold, was born into a Jewish merchant family, received no formal education, and developed into a skilled goldsmith. He married a Jewish woman from Vienna in 1878 and became an Austrian citizen in 1889. There were seven children, and Otto was the second-born and first son, arriving April 3, 1880, in Vienna. His Hebrew name was Schlomoh.

Leopold Weininger became world famous as a goldsmith. He loved music and had a great talent for languages. He was a withdrawn person, keeping his thoughts and feelings to himself. With his family he was exceedingly strict, and he was both loved and feared by his children. His marriage was probably not a happy one.

Very little is known about Otto's relationship with his mother. Otto never mentioned her in his letters. She was an ordinary woman, a housewife and mother, who was beautiful and also had a talent for languages.

The dominant figure in the household was Otto's father. Otto's mother spoiled her children, and they confided in her. But their father was the supreme judge. Eventually, Otto seems to have identified strongly with his father and developed hostility toward his mother. Otto's rejection of his mother may have been a result of identification with his father's views, but Otto was possibly strongly attracted to his mother, and his later attitudes were a reaction against these incestuous desires. Otto seems to have developed into a latent homosexual, latent perhaps because of the negative attitudes of his culture toward homosexuality and because of a lack of opportunities for homosexual experiences.

Otto showed promise early, speaking quite well by the age of fourteen months. He graduated from secondary school in 1898, more learned than his peers. He knew Latin and Greek, spoke German, French, English, Italian, Spanish and Norwegian, and had read extensively in philosophy and literature. He was rather independent of his teachers, even critical of them, and very self-confident, perhaps showing evidence of narcissism and grandiosity in his self-admiration.

His views toward women and Jews soon became very hostile. In his book Sex and Character, published in 1903, Otto described women as the lowest possible level of existence, so that even the best woman is grossly inferior to the worst man, justifying this with a pseudo-biological and psychological rationale.

Otto's parents had never kept a Jewish home or participated in Jewish ceremonies. In fact his father was also anti-semitic. Two of his sisters became Christians, and Otto too rejected the Jewish religion and converted to Christianity in 1902. In his book Sex and Character, Otto described Judaism as an inferior religion as compared to Christianity, equating the Jewish religion with the femininity he so despised. It is relevant to note in this context that anti-semitism was rife in Vienna during Otto's childhood and adolescent years. By 1895, two-thirds of the city council was clearly anti-semitic, and there was talk of excluding the Jews from commerce.

Otto's father had encouraged Otto's study of languages and introduced him to music, first taking him to concerts when Otto was six. His father wanted him to continue the study of languages with a view to entering the diplomatic service, but Otto entered the University of Vienna instead. He attended lectures in several departments, but he focussed on philosophy and psychology. In 1900 at the age of twenty, he attended a psychology congress in Paris, and his contributions to the discussions were noted in the formal congress proceedings. There was no book, concert or theatrical performance about which Otto did not have an opinion. He firmly believed that he was destined to become a genius.

He worked feverishly on his doctoral thesis, neglecting his food and his health. Though he was awarded a doctorate in 1902, Otto overestimated the value and the importance of his contribution. He tried to find a publisher for his thesis, unsuccessfully at first. He showed the thesis to Freud, who thought it quite poor. His thesis was entitled Sex and Character, and on the same day he received his doctorate, Otto joined the Protestant faith.

Otto then moved out from home so that he could pursue his studies more intensively, for example, working at night, a practice which had disturbed his father. He supported himself by working as a private tutor, revising and extending the ideas in his thesis, eventually completing the manuscript for his book of the same title.

From his university years on, signs of a psychiatric illness began to appear. His joining the Protestant faith, perhaps meant as tactic to give his life meaning, seems not to have made him any happier. His introspection seems to have contributed to his self-absorption and to his growing depression. As his reading began to extend to morality, he began to see himself more and more as wicked and sinful. Gradually he grew to hate himself. His sexual desires seem to have especially distressed him.

In his book, Sex and Character, he divides women into "mothers" and "prostitutes," a not uncommon view, but a view which makes nice women unavailable sexually. There is no evidence of loves or lovers in Otto's life, but Otto may have visited prostitutes for sexual satisfaction. In April, 1903, Otto made the decision to remain sexually abstinent.

In 1902, after receiving his doctorate, he accepted some money from his father to travel throughout Europe, returning to Vienna in September 1902. This trip seems not to have helped his growing depression at all, and his friends noted his growing distress. On the night of November 20, 1902, he talked to a friend (Arthur Gerber) about killing himself, and Gerber stayed up the whole night in order to prevent Otto from doing so.

Otto may have begun to suffer from schizophrenia. He may have had hallucinations (hearing dogs barking), and he withdrew more and more from others. Otto's disorder also has elements of manic-depressive disorder, a disorder which is not without occasional hallucinations and delusional thinking.

Otto worked constantly on his book, writing by day and, using candles, by night. It was accepted by a small publishing house in March 1903, and the first copies appeared at the end of May.

Most people ignored the book. Several praised it, especially those to whom its anti-semitism appealed, and several criticized it severely. He was even accused of stealing the ideas in it. Otto's psychological state grew worse after the book appeared. His feelings of sinfulness grew, and his depression was worsened by the indifferent or unfriendly reception given to his book. In the summer he travelled to Italy where he remained depressed and suicidal. He returned to Vienna in September 1903 and, after staying for five days with his parents, rented a room in the house in which Beethoven had lived. He moved there on October 3. The next morning letters arrived at his brother's and father's homes announcing his suicide. His brother rushed over to Otto's apartment, had a locksmith open the door and found Otto dying from a bullet wound in the chest. He was rushed to a hospital but died there that morning.

It is possible simply to dismiss Otto's suicide as that

of a depressed schizophrenic. However, his suicide occurred soon after the publication and rejection of the book which he hoped would bring him recognition. He had also failed to build a mature personal and interpersonal existence. Burdened by a deep sense of sin and continual depression, alienated from others because of both his schizoid tendencies and the conflict between his conscious and unconscious sexual desires, Otto seemed destined to lead an unhappy life alone. Perhaps the failure of his book in this context was sufficient to lead him to a decision to commit suicide?

21. ANNE SEXTON:

PULITZER PRIZE-WINNING POET

Anne Sexton was born as Anne Harvey on November 9, 1928, in Newton, Massachusetts, the third of three daughters. Her father, Ralph, born in 1900, worked in the wool business and eventually established his own firm, and her grandfather was a banker who suffered a psychiatric breakdown under the stress of his business. Anne's father had a younger sister who attempted suicide in her twenties and eventually committed suicide in 1975.

Anne's mother, Mary Gray, born in 1901, was the only child of the editor and publisher of the Lewiston Evening Journal. After her junior year at Wellesley College, she met Ralph Harvey and quit college to marry him.

Of the three children, the eldest, Jane, became Daddy's girl, and she committed suicide in 1983 with sleeping pills. Blanche was seen as the clever child, while Anne was the baby of the family. A nurse helped with the family, and she stayed until Ralph Harvey's death, becoming like an aunt to the three girls. The parents were very close, and the children used to think up ways to gain their parents' attention such as writing them notes or leaving drawings on their parents' pillows.

Anne's father drank heavily, and when drunk he was often irascible. In particular, he used to insult Anne, saying for example that her acne disgusted him and that he could not eat his food with her at the table. Later, in therapy, Anne said that her father sexually molested her. However, her therapist (Martin Orne) noted that her account varied each time she recalled it, and he concluded that it probably had not happened. Orne suggested that the incident was a metaphor for Anne's experience of her father during this period. Anne's mother also drank, but regarded herself as a drunk rather than an alcoholic like her husband. Ralph Harvey finally sought treatment and gave up drinking in 1950.

When Anne was eleven, she was hospitalized for constipation, and her mother showed great anxiety over Anne's bowel movements, threatening her with a colostomy if she was not regular! Her father's aunt, Nana, moved in at this time, and Anne spent almost all of her spare time with Nana. However, after a couple of years, Nana suddenly lost her hearing and became quite child-like in her behavior. After some episodes of violence, Nana was given electroconvulsive therapy at a psychiatric hospital and eventually placed in a clinic. Around this time too, Anne's paternal grandfather had his second breakdown and was hospitalized. Later Anne came to think that maybe she had caused Nana's breakdown and that one day she would break down too.

In junior high school, Anne had many friends and began to take an interest in her appearance. Anne had a steady boy friend, Jack, from eighth grade into high school, and even at sixteen Anne and her friends went to bars and dances. Their favorite drink was Singapore Slings. To calm Anne down, her parents sent her to girl's boarding school. Nevertheless, Anne got engaged to Jack, but he broke off the engagement soon afterwards, leaving Anne heartbroken. Anne's time at high school was full of activities — swimming, basketball, cheerleading, theater and poetry. Her father liked her poems but always told Anne that she was not as brilliant as her mother. Anne's mother was jealous of her daughter, and her hostility led Anne to stop writing for ten years.

After the private high school, Anne went to the Garland School in Boston. She quickly became engaged again, but in the summer she met Alfred Sexton, known as Kayo, fell in love with him, slept with him, broke her engagement, and, thinking that she was pregnant and with the consent of her mother, eloped to get married in North Carolina in August, 1948. Kayo went back to Colgate where he was an undergraduate, but he dropped out at Thanksgiving, and the Sextons moved in with Kayo's parents. Kayo got a job in the wool business, while Anne did some modelling. They found an apartment, and soon Anne fell in love with husband of a couple with whom they were friendly. Nothing developed from this, but Anne did consider divorce at the time and took an overdose of sleeping pills while others were close by who could save her. Her mother suggested she seek counseling with Dr. Martha Brunner-Orne, the psychiatrist who had treated Anne's father for alcoholism.

At the start of the Korean War in 1950, Kayo joined the naval reserve and was shipped overseas. Anne soon began dating other men, but her mother found out and persuaded Anne to join Kayo in San Francisco. Once there, she became pregnant and came back to Massachusetts to give birth. Linda was born July 21, 1953. Kayo returned three days later to take up civilian life again. He joined Ralph Harvey's business as a salesman. A second daughter, Joy, was born August 4, 1955.

Anne felt very constrained by the geographic closeness of her parents and her in-laws and by having Kayo work for her father. Anne was sensitive to the criticism from both sets of parents, and she and Kayo dreamed of leaving the area but never did.

Soon after the birth of Joy, Anne had what appears to be a postpartum depression. She consulted with Dr. Brunner-Orne who gave her medications and counseling. A few months later, Anne began to fear that she might harm the children. She suffered anxiety attacks, especially when Kayo was away on business, and was physically abusive to her daughters.

Eventually, Dr. Brunner-Orne recommended hospitalization at a private clinic. Anne was released in August, 1956, after a stay of three weeks. It was decided that Anne would see Dr. Brunner-Orne's son for psychotherapy, and Anne saw Dr. Martin Orne for the next eight years. Linda, now three, went to stay with Anne's sister, Blanche, for five months. Joy went to stay with Anne's mother-in-law, Billie, for the next three years.

Anne did not improve quickly. In November, she overdosed with barbiturates during Kayo's absence but called Billie to rescue her. Orne put her in a psychiatric hospital for five weeks, and Anne called this a psychotic breakdown and thought that she was possibly insane. Orne, then and later, did not consider Anne psychotic. He eventually diagnosed her as a hysterical neurotic. One problem in therapy was that Anne forgot much of what transpired in each session, and she seemed to have a tendency to fall into "trances" easily. Eventually Orne had her make notes after sessions and listen to tapes of the sessions.

Early in treatment, Orne suggested that Anne write about her experiences in treatment, and Anne began to write poetry again. After another suicide attempt in May 1957 (following her mother's mastectomy for cancer which her mother blamed on the stress created by Anne), Orne strongly urged that her poems might help others who had similar problems, and Anne began to consider poetry as a possible vocation. In 1957, she brought over sixty poems to Orne for him to read. She decided then to enroll in a poetry workshop held at the Boston Center for Adult Education taught by John Holmes, a professor at Tufts University (whose first wife had committed suicide). Anne, timid at first, soon felt at home there and stayed two years. Her first poem was published in a local magazine in April, 1958. Thereafter, with surprising persistence, Anne submitted her poems for publication, recording the rejections, but never giving up.

Anne requested a third meeting each week with Orne, and he agreed provided that she paid for it (instead of her father-in-law). Anne did so by getting a job selling cosmetics door-to-door. Billie was now even more involved with Anne's life, taking care of Anne's family whenever Anne was too upset to do so.

Anne met a fellow writer, Maxine Kumin, at the poetry workshop, and they became close friends, calling each other every day to discuss their writing. They went to poetry readings together and socialized with their families. Anne also found a lover among her classmates.

By mid-1958, Anne had sixty poems in circulation, seeking publication. The Christian Science Monitor accepted two for their July issue, and she soon had acceptances from the Antioch Review, Harper's, and The New Yorker. Anne was now taking antidepressants, and Joy came home for longer and longer periods. But at the same time, Kayo became increasingly upset by Anne's devotion to her poetry and her accompanying neglect of her family. The arguments often turned into physical fights, followed by remorse on Kayo's part. Anne eventually came to see that she wanted the physical attacks in part as punishment for her poor behavior. Later that year (1958), Anne's father had a stroke, and her mother's cancer metastasized. In November, Anne went into her therapist's clinic for several days.

In September, 1958, Anne joined Robert Lowell's poetry class at Boston University. At the end of 1958, the Hudson Review accepted a 240-line poem, and Anne began planning her first book. Anne showed great professionalism as a poet. She worked hard on redrafting poems, courting the editors of journals, and publishing poems serially in journals before they appeared in book form, in short, actively promoting herself. She also began to develop a public image which led to her becoming one of the most memorable performers on the poetry circuit.

Anne continued to write productively and receive acclaim for her work. Poems and books appeared regularly, and prizes and honors were awarded to her, including a fellowship at the Radcliffe Institute, the Levinson prize from Poetry in 1962, a traveling fellowship from the American Academy of Arts and Letters in 1963 (for which she went to Europe with a female companion in 1963 and with Kayo in 1964), a travel grant from the International Congress of Cultural Freedom in 1964 (for which she took Kayo on a safari to Kenya), fellowship in the Royal Society of Literature in 1964, the Shelley Memorial Prize from the Poetry Society of America and a Pulitzer Prize in 1967, a Guggenheim Foundation grant in 1969, an honorary doctorate from Tufts University in 1970, and a visiting professorship at Colgate University in 1972. Her poetry readings increased in popularity until she was demanding $1000 for each reading.

Not all was successful. Anne tried to publish short stories and a novel, but failed in this. She tried several plays, but only one was performed, Mercy Street in 1968 (though she was more successful with a musical ensemble which set her poetry readings to music). In addition, the British reception for her poetry and her readings was not anywhere near as positive as the American response.

Writing dominated her life, and she neglected chores, so that Kayo and her daughters, as well as her mother-in-law, all helped keep the household running while Anne wrote, traveled or stayed in psychiatric clinics. Eventually Anne's self-centeredness led her to parentalize her daughters so that they had to take care of her, and she used them for her comfort and to satisfy her sexual needs, even to the point of sexually molesting them, with the result that they sought psychotherapy later in their lives.

Anne continued to take lovers to the point that her behavior seems promiscuous. In 1960, she had an abortion because she was not certain that the child was Kayo's. She also had a brief homosexual encounter with a friend in 1965.

By 1966, Anne was thinking of divorcing Kayo. Anne realized that she was dependent upon Kayo for her stable home life, but she also resented his lack of support for her career as a poet. By 1969, Kayo was becoming violent again. His wife was brazen about her affairs, talking to lovers on the telephone when Kayo was home, and they were drunk by dinner-time most evenings. She moved out in January, 1973, but, after a court hearing in March, Kayo moved out of their house, leaving it to Anne. Anne found a live-in couple to help with the household, but they fled from her after a few months. Her daughters were growing up and away from her, and Anne found few new lovers.

Although Anne developed a public persona, witty and extraverted, she was tremendously insecure about meeting others and suffered great anxiety before public talks and parties. Eventually, she took to drinking alcohol to calm herself before public appearances. However, soon after her breakdown in the early 1950s, Anne used to experience panic whenever she had to leave the house, and so her development as a poet certainly eased the level of her anxiety. Anne liked to have someone with her when she went to sleep, Kayo or some lover, even after she started taking sleeping pills. By the 1970s, Anne was abusing both alcohol and medications.

Anne needed, and was lucky to have, a series of colleagues or mentors, other poets, with whom she would correspond voluminously about work, as well as close-neighbors like Maxine Kumin and, later, Lois Ames, with whom to share ideas and trips. After she fell and broke her hip in 1966, a neighbor, Joan Smith, helped nurse Anne and continued to help Anne for the rest of her life.

Anne continued to attempt suicide, stay at clinics (which she also used as writing retreats), and remain in psychotherapy. In 1974, after seven years of working with Anne, Orne moved to Philadelphia, and he was replaced by a therapist who committed professional misconduct by becoming Anne's lover. He eventually rejected Anne as a lover when his wife found out about the affair. When this therapeutic relationship ended in 1969, Anne transferred to a third therapist, this time a women, who demanded that Anne break off her occasional sessions with Orne whenever he returned to Boston. In late 1973, this third therapist, angered by Anne, ended the relationship. Anne began to visit a social worker until a replacement therapist could be found, but in October 1974 she committed suicide.

In 1964, after a severe breakdown, Anne stayed in Massachusetts General Hospital, where she was given an antidepressant (imipramine) but switched to a phenothiazine (Thorazine). She took this for the rest of her life, but she felt that it destroyed her creativity, and so she often went for periods without taking it so that she could write. However, during those periods she would then become quite manic.

Suicide fascinated Anne. She attempted suicide many times herself and for many years carried barbiturates in her purse with everywhere in case the mood to die came on her suddenly. She talked to Sylvia Plath in the late 1950s about their earlier suicide attempts, and she was moved by Plath's suicide in 1963. A friend, Ruth Soter, possibly committed suicide in 1964.

Anne suffered several losses in adulthood. Her

mother died in March, 1959, and her father in June, 1959. Her father-in-law was killed in a car crash in 1960. Her sister-in-law was killed in a car accident on her honeymoon in 1969. But most important of all, in 1970, she met a man who claimed to be her real father and persuaded Anne that his affair with her mother had indeed resulted in Anne's conception. Anne's psychological state deteriorated after this disclosure — the first suicide attempt since 1966 and the first clinic stay since 1964.

By the end of 1973, Anne was divorced but regretting it. She was living alone, abusing alcohol and drugs, having difficulty writing, and deserted by her friends who were bored by her problems and who disliked her drunken behavior. She took to phoning friends at all hours. In late 1973, her therapist (her third one) refused to continue in therapy with her, and she began seeing a social worker for counseling. In December 1973, Philip Rahv, an old friend, committed suicide. Anne made two suicide attempts with medications in September, 1973, and two more over the Winter, but she told a friend that car exhaust was the way to die. Sexually lonely, she put personal ads in the local newspaper. She also took religious instruction and contemplated being baptized as an Episcopalian. Nothing seemed to work or to help her. On October 4, she went into her garage, turned the radio on and started the car. She was soon dead.

For Anne Sexton, suicide was almost a way of life. A rough listing of her attempts (all with medications) is 1949, November 1956, May 1957, November 1961, July 1966, August 1970, September 1973 (two), Winter 1973-1974 (two), February 1974, and Spring 1974. Interestingly, she switched methods for her final successful suicidal act.

Anne remained in psychotherapy from 1956 until her death in 1974, and she was hospitalized on many occasions (at least seven times between 1956 and 1964 and at least four more times between 1971 and 1974). She took antidepressants and Thorazine (and suffered from some of the side effects, including Parkinson's symptoms), but she never received electroconvulsive therapy.

Anne fits well with her first therapist's diagnosis of hysteric. She was critically dependent upon attention, succor and love from others. Alone, she panicked and fell into depressions. Like some of R. D. Laing's cases, Anne seemed only to exist when there were others to notice her. Her promiscuity fits well into this pattern. Her decision to divorce Kayo, coming as it did with her daughters growing independence and her mother-in-law's remarriage, was perhaps a mistake. Although her final decline began some time before the divorce, it increased afterwards.

Anne was in psychotherapy from 1956 to 1974, and it is remarkable that it failed to save her or even modify her behavior much at all. Anne was depressed, a substance abuser, promiscuous and prone to trances right to the end. The therapist misconduct is also striking. One therapist used her to satisfy his sexual desires; another demanded that she break with her first therapist (Orne) and then eventually abandoned her.

Her first therapist, Orne, seems to have hit upon the right vocation for Anne in encouraging her to write poetry, much of which was based on her experiences as a psychiatric patient. Anne, along with Robert Lowell and Sylvia Plath, dealt with subject matter long avoided, such as madness and the everyday concerns of normal people, including pregnancy and menstruation. It has been argued that writing poetry enabled Anne to survive longer than she might otherwise have done.

However, Anne remained developmentally immature, perhaps hampered by her parents ignoring her, except for harsh criticism, and her father's drunkenness and abuse. She never grew into a mature person, capable of taking care of herself or others, preferring the role of a dependent child. Finally, having rejected some and having been abandoned by others, she killed herself. Without the attention of others, Anne did not feel as if she really existed. Left alone, death could hardly be worse.

22. ALAN LADD:

TINY!

Ina Ladd, a reserved Englishwoman, gave birth to her only child, Alan Ladd, September 3, 1913, in Hot Springs, Arkansas. She was born in 1888 in West Chester, England, had emigrated to the United States in 1907 and had married in 1912. Her husband, Alan Ladd Sr, was American-born of Scottish ancestry and traveled around as a freelance accountant. He died of a heart attack in front of his family in 1917.

After Alan and a friend accidentally burned down Ina's apartment, Ina took Alan to Oklahoma City where Alan, then seven, was tormented at school and made very few friends. Ina met and married a house painter, James Beaver, there, and they moved to California. It took them three months to drive to Los Angeles in a 1914 Model T Ford, often stopping to work on the way to earn enough money for the trip. In Flagstaff they helped with the harvest, with Alan fetching water and digging tubers. They arrived at a transient auto camp in Pasadena, and Jim Beaver worked as a laborer until he could buy some paint brushes, and he eventually got a job as a painter at a movie studio. They moved first to a tent village, then to a shared house and finally to a garage on a small lot which he and Alan built. They ate simply, often potatoes and cheap mutton, and Alan was never able to eat lamb again for the rest of his life.

Alan got sick with a stomach ailment when he was twelve, perhaps from the years of struggle and malnutrition, and the family moved to small house in the San Fernando Valley for his health. Alan had fallen behind in his learning so that he was the oldest boy in his classes, yet he remained one of the smallest. His classmates nicknamed him Tiny, a name which stuck with him for the rest of his life.

He started work after school when he was fourteen and enrolled in North Hollywood High School when he was sixteen. He did well at athletics and was so good at swimming that there was talk of trying for the 1932 Olympics. He performed in the high school drama productions and, for the first time, but not the last, a movie company saw him and signed him briefly before letting him go. They told him that he was too short (only five foot four).

After graduating from high school in 1934, Alan worked for a local newspaper until he had enough money to open a small hamburger and malt shop. His mother, now middle-aged and drinking too much, helped him with it, but they had to close it after six months. Alan then went to work for Warner Brothers studio as a grip but quit after eight months. Meanwhile, Alan had met a local girl, Midge Harrold, and they secretly married in October, 1936, just after his step-father had died of a heart attack. Midge got pregnant, and so they had to tell her parents. Midge moved into Alan's apartment, and the baby was born on October 20, 1937, Alan Ladd Jr, the future president of Twentieth Century Fox.

Alan was now working for a local radio station as an actor, and his mother, back from a jaunt to San Francisco, moved in with Alan and Midge. She was depressed and drinking heavily, and on November 29, 1937, she poisoned herself with arsenic (in ant paste) and died.

Alan began to gain a reputation as a good radio actor with an extraordinary voice. He performed on the Texaco Star Theater and the Lux Radio Theater and was signed up by an agent, Sue Carol. Sue was born in 1903, worked as an actress, and married three times with one daughter. Sue worked hard on Alan's account and soon found him small parts in movies. From 1939 to 1941 Alan had many, mainly unimpressive, roles. She became friendly with Midge and often had the couple over for parties at her house.

The roles kept coming, and Sue persuaded Alan to take all of them. It kept him visible and provided lots of film clips to show directors and producers. Eventually Alan and Sue fell in love, and Alan left Midge in the Spring of 1941. Midge let him go without a struggle and, though she missed him, never impeded him in his career. Sue had got his salary up from $150 a week to $750 a week when Paramount gave him a role in This Gun For Hire and a long-term contract.

Sue got a divorce in Nevada in March, 1942, and she and Alan were married soon afterwards in Tijuana, Mexico. Alan was twenty-nine and Sue thirty-nine. Once This Gun For Hire was released, it became a huge success, and Alan Ladd became a major star. Although somewhat overwhelmed by his fame, Alan, coached by Sue, established good relations with the press so that the movie magazines (which were very important in those days for a star's career) ran lots of stories on the Ladds (sometimes one a month), all favorable. Alan and Sue were also considerate to the fans, replying to letters and signing autographs. Both Louella Parsons and Hedda Hopper loved the Ladds and printed positive news about them. The press never mentioned their previous marriages or their children despite the fact that Sue's daughter lived with the Ladds and Laddie (Alan's son with Midge) was a frequent visitor, eventually moving in.

Alan was drafted in January 1943, and, after a send-off party from Paramount, went to Fort McArthur in California where he worked making propaganda and training films. His daughter Alana was born in April 1943, and Alan received a medical discharge in November after getting ill several times.

Alan's life settled into a routine. He made a succession of movies, and on the whole they got worse over time, finally ending up as second features at movie houses. His inability to land good roles in good movies stemmed at first from Paramount's policies which demanded that their stars make the kind of movies which the studio thought that the public wanted and which minimized risk. At Paramount, Alan had no control over scripts or directors, even after he went on strike and refused to work for them for four months, after which they gave in and raised his salary. However, after Alan left Paramount to join Warner Brothers where he had story approval and freedom to start his own production company, Alan continued to make poor movies. This suggests that either Alan had poor judgment as far as drama was concerned or that he was so anxious about money that he suspended his judgment and took any role that was offered to him. On the rare occasions in which he found a role he wanted, such as the lead in what was to become Lawrence of Arabia, he was passed over for it. But he also turned down potentially good roles such as one offered him in Giant. Almost every film he was in was severely criticized by movie critics (with the exception of Shane in 1953). Despite the criticism, however, for many years the public loved him. From 1948 to 1950, he was first in the Modern Screen poll.

He accepted contracts to make movies abroad though practically every experience abroad was unpleasant. He would often get injured, miss America, and typically end up in third-rate movies.

Despite the gradual decline in his acting reputation, Alan made a great deal of money, and everything he invested in also made money. He bought a ranch in Hidden Valley south of Santa Barbara which appreciated in value. He built a grand house in Hollywood on North Mapleton Drive. He bought a house in Palm Springs, a second ranch, an office building in Hollywood, and a hardware store, invested in modern art, and hit oil on the Hidden Valley ranch, all of which made money for him.

But he always felt insecure. Alan never thought that he was a good actor, especially after he left the protective care of Paramount. His height also bothered him, especially since it bothered the movie studios. Whereas other short actors had no problems with their height (such as James Cagney), Alan Ladd was always cast as the hero/lover, often opposite women who were as tall or taller than him. Thus, "Tiny" had to stand on platforms or the women stood in ditches when filming. Sometimes others made disparaging remarks about his height. For example, Robert Mitchum was quoted in the press as describing Alan as shrunken up like a dishwasher's hand, so small they could hardly see him.

His personal life with Sue seemed good except for a romantic fling with June Allyson in 1955. There was a row between Sue and June Allyson, and Alan left their home to be by himself for a few days. The Ladds patched things up, and there were never any extramarital affairs again.

Alan drank heavily, but he never arrived on the set drunk. His family later said that his tolerance for alcohol was so low that he could get drunk on very little alcohol. He had trouble sleeping and used sleeping pills washed down by a strong drink. In time, his appearance changed, and he often was overweight and his face bloated. The death of his first wife, Midge, in 1957, depressed him. His fellow actors and actresses in the 1950s described him as melancholic.

By the 1960s, he had fewer fans. His movies were not popular, and they were sometimes given second billing. He failed to adapt to the changing tastes of movie goers, and his ventures into productions for television failed. His insomnia and depressions grew worse, though he was still financially secure. Working on the next movie, no matter how bad it might be, seemed to alleviate his depressions briefly.

In 1962, a friend, Van Heflin, advised Alan to try psychotherapy, but the idea was too terrifying, although he talked to Heflin about the loss of his good looks, his lack of self-esteem and his fears of diminished sexual potency. In November of 1962, Alan drove out to the Hidden Valley ranch alone and was found in the morning unconscious from a bullet in the chest. This incident was labeled an accident, and Alan said he had tripped over his dogs while carrying the gun.

The deaths of Hollywood friends, acquaintances and co-stars (such as Gail Russell, Marilyn Monroe, and Dick Powell) increased his melancholy.

His death occurred while he was staying alone at his Palm Springs house. He was depressed — sleeping poorly, drinking heavily, watching television and talking to friends on the telephone. He was found at 3:30 in the afternoon on January 29, 1964, by his butler, dead from an overdose of sleeping pills and alcohol. The coroner ruled the death an accident.

Alan Ladd's career was moving downhill fast, and this fed into his insecurities about himself as an actor. Public failure meant artistic failure. There is a suggestion that his marriage, which once had helped him to success, was no longer a source of satisfaction for him. His childhood experience of poverty led him to do almost anything to make money, despite the money he had accumulated, and he seemed driven in this. Alan was devoted to his children and proud of them, but this was not sufficient to make life worth living.

His death may have been an accident, but the timing and the circumstances suggests suicide. He isolated himself in Palm Springs so that no one could intervene to save him. His depression was getting worse, and yet he was unwilling to seek professional help. The public adoration was no longer there to bolster his self-esteem. And he had, of course, the memory of his mother taking arsenic in mid-life when her problems seemed no longer bearable.

23. CHARLES BOYER:

THE SCREEN LOVER WHO DIED FOR

LOVE

Charles Boyer was born in Figeac, in the pastoral southwest of France on August 28, 1899. His father, Maurice Boyer, had moved to Figeac on the death of his first wife and opened a bicycle shop, where he met and married a thirty year-old spinster, Louise Durand. Maurice Boyer eventually sold farming equipment and moved into coal and grain sales. Charles was their only child.

Charles was a precocious boy in his studies, reading Shakespeare while his fellow pupils were still learning their alphabet. He was introverted and showed little interest in boyish games or athletics. Charles's father had consumption, but nevertheless his death in 1909 came as shock to the family. Louise sold off the business and focussed her energies on her only child. She paid for violin lessons for him and foresaw a career in medicine or the law. But Charles was smitten as child by the cinema and by the theater, and he resolved to be an actor, playwright and director. As a teenager, he devised a version of Macbeth for himself and his friends to act in. A class essay on Molière won a provincial prize.

In his teenage years, he developed into a handsome young man. When the First World War broke out, he worked as an orderly in a local hospital. He entered the Collège Campollion, near Figeac, but neglected his studies. He devoted much time instead to entertaining the hospitalized troops. Devising these entertainments made him realize that he did not like writing but that he did like acting. In 1918, he was recruited to play a small part in a film being made nearby, and the director persuaded Charles's mother that her son should go to Paris to become an actor. His mother allowed him to go on condition he enroll for studies at the Sorbonne.

Charles neglected his studies there in favor of making contacts in the theater world. After many rejections, his roommate recommended Charles for a major part in play in which the leading actor had fallen ill twelve hours before the opening performance. He learned the part in one day and became an overnight celebrity. The leading actor took over when he recovered, but Charles used his success to persuade the producer to get him admittance into the prestigious Conservatoire National Supérieur de Musique et de Déclamation de Paris.

He studied diligently there (and graduated), at the same time accepting roles in plays and films. Although he loved acting on the stage, he saw that there was more money to be earned in films, and so he willingly took film parts. He was soon familiar to Parisian playgoers and, through his films, throughout France. He became the highest paid actor on the French legitimate stage and performed in nine countries.

Though he could speak French, German, Italian, Spanish and Portuguese, his English was poor. Nevertheless, he was persuaded to go to Hollywood for the first time in 1929 to make a French version of a film recently filmed in English using American actors. On Charles's next trip to Hollywood, Irving Thalberg took charge of him, providing him with an English tutor so that Charles could act in the English versions of films. However, there was lots of idle time, and Charles took up smoking, becoming a four-pack-a-day chain smoker. In 1931, he worked in his first American film, The Magnificent Lie. It was a flop. Charles returned to France feeling that he had failed twice in Hollywood. Back in France, he returned to the stage and films, falling in love with a Anglo-French actress, Alice Fields, who rejected his proposal of marriage.

MGM asked Charles to return to Hollywood for Red-Headed Woman which also starred Jean Harlow. The film helped propel Charles into the public eye, but Irving Thalberg had a nervous breakdown and went off to Europe and MGM cut back on productions. So in 1932, for the third time, Charles returned to France in gloom. Back in France though he was still a star.

By 1933, the German artists who were being persecuted by the Nazis were on their way to America, and Paris was their first stop. Charles met many of them and worked with them. One of them, Erich Charell, planned to go to Hollywood to make Caravan and persuaded Charles to be in it.

This time, Charles's life in Hollywood was happier. In January 1934, he met a British actress there, Pat Paterson, born in 1910 in Bradford, England. Twenty-two days after they met, they drove to Yuma, Arizona, and got married. Charles was thirty-four, Pat twenty-three.

Pat wanted to have a film career, but her films were not successes and the studios gradually lost interest in her. Though very disappointed, this removed a source of friction in the marriage, for it was proving difficult to advance both careers and stay happily married. Charles hated to be away from Pat, and she was an important source of support for him after unsuccessful films. He also held rather traditional ideas about what a wife's role should be. Pat had a contract with Fox Studios but, after they folded in 1935, other studios did not offer her work, and so the conflict between the two careers was resolved.

Charles continued to make films on both sides of the Atlantic. He refused to sign up with any studio, remaining independent, and managed in most years to earn a very good income, roughly $100,000 for each film by 1935. Perhaps 1937 was a peak year for his career. He received an Oscar nomination for his role in Conquest, in which he starred with Greta Garbo, and a European film Mayerling was a success in America that year too.

In 1936, the Boyers bought a house in Beverly Hills and settled down. They were very sociable and befriended any English and French film people who came to Hollywood. Yet they also kept private. Their home was off-limits to the press, and Charles appeared infrequently in the fan magazines. Surprisingly for a Hollywood couple, Charles remained happily in love with Pat for the rest of their lives. Despite starring in films with almost every leading lady of the era, and despite his reputation in films as lover, he never had an affair. He invested his money wisely and soon was quite wealthy. They applied for United States citizenship (and become citizens in 1942) and, since they seemed to have difficulty conceiving a child, inquired about adoption.

They travelled to France on September 1939, the day Hitler attacked Poland. Charles joined the French army and sent Pat to England. He was assigned to the 37th Artillery to perform switchboard duties at one of the Maginot Line's fortifications. However, the French authorities decided that Charles would be better as an emissary for them in America, and he was mustered out and urged to return to America.

Back in Hollywood, he made efforts to get his friends to safety after the fall of France, frequently flying to Lisbon to make arrangements. He made radio broadcasts for Voice of America. He founded a French Research Foundation to document French contributions to culture but, during the war, he focussed its efforts on documenting the French involvement in the war. By 1941, he was smoking six packs a day and exhausted. He had heart palpitations, and his doctor ordered him to cut down his smoking and slow down. Thereafter, he made only one, or at most two, films a year. Then Pat got pregnant, and Michael was born on December 9, 1943.

Charles returned to France for a while after the war and put much effort into saving from execution and imprisonment those actors and directors accused of collaborating with the Nazis.

Back in America, Charles returned to the stage in New York City, appearing in Sartre's Red Gloves and helping to put on and act in several other plays. He also appeared in some thirty films made in America and in Europe. His changing interests led him to sell the house in California and move into a suite in the Hotel Pierre in New York City. As well as his changing interests, Charles was upset by the persecution of Ingrid Bergman for having an illegitimate child and by the cooperation of the film industry with the Committee on Un-American Activities. He and Pat bought an apartment in Paris, a house in London, and a home on the island of Ischia in the Mediterranean (where the family gathered every summer to paint).

Michael decided as a teenager that he wanted to work in television as a producer. Charles had seen the potential of this new medium and had formed a successful production company with some friends which produced Four Star Playhouse and The Rogues among others. Michael was the producer for The Rogues and, after it was cancelled in 1964, it was expected he would soon find other projects. But Michael had little talent and even less training. New projects did not appear. He fell in love but, when his lover told him that she wanted to break their relationship off, he went into his den and shot himself — September 23, 1965.

The Boyers never recovered from Michael's suicide. They sold their houses and retired to Geneva. Charles did make a few more films. Probably the activity helped him survive. His health grew worse, and in 1977 Charles and Pat flew to New York for medical check-ups. Charles was told he needed a prostatectomy, and Pat was discovered to have advanced cancer of the colon and liver. Charles decided not to tell Pat, but he moved them to Scottsdale, Arizona, since the climate was better there for her. She died there on August 24, 1978. Charles did not go to her funeral in California. He got their house in order and killed himself with an overdose of barbiturates on August 26, 1978, two days before his seventy-ninth birthday.

24. GIG YOUNG:

THEY SHOOT ACTORS, DON'T THEY?

Byron Barr was born in St. Cloud, Minnesota, on November 4, 1913, the third of three children and an unplanned baby. His father, stern and distant, ran a pickling and preserving company, his mother was repressed and neurasthenic, and his older brother domineering. Byron was close only to his sister Genevieve and remained so all of his life. In his early years, his mother often took to her room sick, and her step-sister, Jessie, came to live with the Barrs to help with the children. Byron grew close to Jessie, but eventually he realized that Jessie liked his older brother, Don, better than she liked him. Thus, both female caretakers had rejected him.

Byron developed a number of psychosomatic complaints, including convulsions and a stiff neck, and at elementary school he soon fell behind and was placed with the group of slow learners. His second grade teacher sadistically beat him, and he had to repeat second-grade.

Byron rarely expressed his pain or resentment. He learned to hide behind a smiling countenance, revealing his true feelings only to his sister. His older brother had worked in his father's company successfully, and Byron too was forced to work there after school. There he failed too. The foreman fired him, not realizing he was the boss's son, and his father rehired him but at reduced pay. As a teenager, Byron was attracted by the movies, and he got a job as an usher at the local theater so that he could see the films. He day-dreamt about being an actor.

At the Technical High School, Byron was a good-looking young man, and he was popular, even getting elected class president. Since his father's business was profitable, Byron had lots of nice clothes and use of the family car, and he developed more confidence.

The Depression brought hard times. The father's company folded, and he took a job as a food broker in Washington, DC, while Byron stayed in St. Cloud to take care of his ailing mother. As he finished his junior year of high school, his father summoned the family to Washington, and so in April, 1932, Byron drove his sick and depressed mother to join his father.

Since his father lived far from the high school there, Byron persuaded his parents to let him board near his school. His landlady, Mrs. Harry Kaines, liked him and became his surrogate mother. She was thrilled by his athletic success, and one of her tenants got him a job at the local drug store. When his parents moved to North Carolina, Byron persuaded them to let him stay with Mrs. Kaines. Mrs. Kaines helped get him a job as a ballroom dancing instructor and encouraged him to join the local semi-professional theater group. At this time too, he had the gap in his front teeth closed and a testicular inflammation forced him to have a vasectomy. Finally in 1939, he set out for California, hitch-hiking across America.

Arriving in California, Byron got work at a gas station and building scenery at an acting school. He auditioned successfully at the Pasadena Playhouse and acted in many plays. There he met a fellow actress, Sheila Stapler, with whom he fell in love. Sheila was very nurturing and was happy to defer to Byron. They slipped off to Las Vegas in August 1940 to marry.

In 1941, Byron was asked to take a screen test for Warner Brothers, and he was signed up at $75 a week. He worked diligently there, but also remained a family man, spending time with Sheila and working on his house.

When America entered the war in 1941, the movie studios lost many male actors, and Warner Brothers persuaded Byron not to enlist. They upgraded the roles given to Byron, and he took as his name the role he played in The Gay Sisters, Gig Young. His next film was Old Acquaintance with Bette Davis, and Gig and Bette had an affair, a portent that Gig was most likely not going to be a stable husband.

Gig finally had to enlist, joining the Coast Guard in 1943, but Sheila moved with him until he was shipped off to sea as a pharmacist's mate in late 1944, just after his mother died. He got malaria soon afterwards, and was released on July 4, 1945. Warner Brothers threw a welcome back party for him and several other returning actors, and Gig hoped that his fortunes would improve. However, Warner Brothers gave him second-string and unflattering roles in many of their run-of-the-mill movies, and the momentum of his career slowed.

He grew closer to Sophie Rosenstein, a drama coach for the studio (the two couples socialized a lot together), and Gig and Sophie fell in love. Sophie worked hard to encourage Gig and to help him land better roles. She urged him to act on the stage in order to expand his horizons, but in the summer of 1947 while he was appearing in Biography with the La Jolla Playhouse, Warner Brothers dropped his option. His brother Don died in September 1949 of tubercular meningitis and, although he had always resented his brother, Gig was depressed by this loss. His marriage to Sheila deteriorated, and, as his drinking increased, Gig took to breaking the furniture during their rows. They separated after Christmas 1948 and divorced in 1949. Gig persuaded Sophie to divorce her husband, and they married on January 1, 1951.

Working as an independent, Gig let his agent sign him up for mediocre roles and, after getting and breaking a contract with Columbia, he hardly worked in 1949 and 1950. He freelanced a few roles in 1951, but then signed with the Louis Shurr Agency. He obtained a good part and turned in a good performance in Come Fill The Cup for which he was nominated as best supporting actor in 1952. But then he signed with MGM who put him in mediocre films, and his career fizzled again.

He failed to insist on better roles, and Sophie could not help him since she was diagnosed with cervical cancer just three months after their marriage. Gig held the knowledge from Sophie and spent most of his energy taking care of her. By October 1952, she spent most of her time in bed, and Gig stayed home, reading to her and holding her hand. She had to be hospitalized in October 1952, and she died on November 10. Gig was devastated and seriously depressed. He drank heavily and took Miltown to help him sleep. When his contract with MGM expired, Gig decided to go to New York to act on the stage. He got his first part in Oh Men! Oh Women! in 1953 and received great reviews. He also began to recover from his bereavement, and had two affairs. First there was Sherry Britton, a big-time stripper, to whom Gig proposed marriage. She refused. Elaine Stritch was acting in a show in a neighboring theater and met Gig at a party she gave. He stayed overnight to help her wash dishes and slept in a separate bed. The virgin Elaine was impressed, and they began dating. Soon she fell in love with him, and Gig tried to have his first marriage annulled and planned to convert to Roman Catholicism in order to marry her. After they went back to Hollywood where Gig had a role in a movie, the church found out that he had been baptized as a Methodist and that annulment was impossible. Their relationship broke up soon after.

For a while, Gig shuttled back and forth between New York and Hollywood, but he found few good roles and took any that were offered. He met Elizabeth

Montgomery, and they married in December 1956. Gig had his vasectomy reversed so they could have children, and Gig finally had a good role in Teacher's Pet which got him a second Oscar nomination. This led to lots of offers, and Gig and Liz moved to the West Coast. Gig was still drinking heavily, but Liz seemed to be able match him in this.

Returning to the East Coast for Under The Yum Yum Tree, Gig began to show signs of what later became a severe trouble, his inability to master the lines for a play. As his marriage with Liz deteriorated, Gig found a new mother-figure, Doris Rich, a character actress in her mid-sixties, a relationship which made Liz feel threatened. Gig next had a liaison with Sophia Loren during the filming of Five Miles To Midnight in 1962, but then became suspicious about Liz having affairs. Eventually, Liz obtained a Mexican divorce in March 1963.

Gig drowned his sorrows in alcohol, but he soon met Elaine Whitman who was, at the time, selling real estate. Soon after their affair began, Elaine discovered she was pregnant, and Gig, overjoyed, married her, though friends thought it was a terrible match. Elaine was twenty-eight, Gig forty-nine. Elaine and Gig had a daughter, Jennifer, in April, 1964. Elaine tried domesticity, while Gig tried AA, dieted and acquired toupees for his receding hairline. His failing career soon brought financial worries. He starred in a television series for a year, The Rogues, but it was cancelled. He was in a successfully touring company of The Music Man but had to sell his luxurious house and move into a smaller place.

Gig's paranoia now focussed on Elaine, and he tapped his own telephone line so as to record her conversations. Gig persuaded Elaine to go into counseling with him, but he chose an unqualified therapist. Elaine refused to continue, and then Gig went to Vancouver for a course of LSD therapy. Their arguments about Gig's drinking continued, and Elaine divorced Gig in July, 1967.

Gig was now getting almost no offers for films, and appeared only in touring companies and occasionally in New York City. An affair there with a young actress was ruined by his drinking and his impotence and, though she would have married him, Gig refused to consider it. At this nadir in his life, he was recommended for the role of Rockie Gravo in They Shoot Horses, Don't They? and he won an Oscar for best supporting actor in 1970 for it.

And then his career plummeted again! Elaine sued him in court for more alimony and child support, and Gig tried to deny paternity for Jennifer. He lost in court after five years of legal battles which created great animosity between them, and Gig never saw Jennifer again. Furthermore, public opinion turned against him. Then in his touring company for Harvey, there was great conflict between Gig and other actors and, though the production was a success, Gig acquired a reputation for being difficult. The stress of this experience led to a severe neurodermatitis on his face.

Next, Gig was hired for a film, Blazing Saddles, but he had problems learning the lines and his anxiety caused him to collapse on the set. He was fired. His reputation for being unreliable grew. Luckily though, he found another supporter, Harriette Vine Douglas, a woman in her fifties, who became his friend, confidante and lover. She protected him in every way she could, and he often hid out with her for months.

He tried plastic surgery for his aging face, but the surgeon botched the operation and Gig required remedial surgery. His teeth bothered him so that, on tour with On A Clear Day You Can See Forever, he could hardly eat. After his weight dropped from 185 to 145, he had all of his teeth recapped. In 1972, he developed numbness in his feet and was treated for circulatory problems and had his gallbladder removed. After this, he stayed with Harriette for almost a year.

In 1974 and 1975, he appeared in five movies. He went on the wagon, relying more heavily on Valium and Placidyl, and made a television movie which became a series. He had problems learning the lines and hired a good psychologist who helped him. But after the series, when the psychologist tried to get Gig to deal with his underlying and chronic problems (his alcoholism, sexual impotence and paranoia), Gig quit therapy. Gig had his teeth redone and had plastic surgery on his chin and eyelids.

Back in New York, he was fired from Arthur Miller's The Archbishop's Ceiling because he could not remember his lines, despite help from his voice-coach there, Bert Knapp, who had managed also to become Gig's therapist though unqualified for such a role. In 1977, Gig went to Hong Kong to make a kung fu film (his last film) and met Kim Schmidt.

Kim was the thirty year-old script girl for the film, and they soon became involved. Their relationship was volatile, and Kim desperately tried to get Gig to stop drinking. Gig returned to New York alone, but the relationship improved by telephone, and Kim joined him in New York in October 1977.

He signed up to perform in a college production of Long Day's Journey Into Night at the University of Memphis, where his memorization problems led to the first performance ending forty-five minutes early as Gig forgot large chunks of his lines. Back in New York, Gig and Kim quarreled, made up, split and got back together again. Gig proposed marriage, but Kim resisted. In May, Gig appeared drunk on stage when introducing a friend's concert performance, and his voice-coach/psychotherapist broke his relationship with Gig. In June, 1978, Gig and Kim went to Edmonton where Gig was to perform in Nobody Loves An Albatross. Gig had fantasies of taking the show on tour, but friends who came to advise him on it thought the production was terrible.

Back in New York, Gig and Kim bought an apartment and, on September 27, 1978, finally married. Money was scarce because of their heavy spending and the expense of fixing up the apartment.

Perhaps it was the fears of aging and sickness, perhaps his sexual impotence or arguments over money, perhaps it was a fight over the will (with Kim wanting all the inheritance and Gig wanting to split it between Kim and his sister), or perhaps his withdrawal from alcohol and drugs led to an acute psychosis? He did telephone Harriette on October 18 to beg her to come to New York and take him back to Hollywood. She refused.

On October 19, 1978, Gig shot Kim in the back of the head and then shot himself in the head. After the deaths, no barbiturates or alcohol was found in Gig's system. The apartment had two bottles of wine, seven tablets of Oxazepam and several bottles of vitamins.

Gig Young was a man whose life disintegrated slowly, interspersed with occasional successes and critical turning points. From a difficult childhood, filled with rejection, he built a career but lacked the skills to manage it well. As he progressed from relationship to relationship and from performance to performance, his alcohol abuse worsened, his distrust of others and paranoia worsened, and his violent behavior escalated. The eventual end of his life was hardly predictable. Murder-suicide is rare. But a decline was inevitable, perhaps into bankrupt alcoholism.

But there were also critical turning points. What if Sophie, his second wife, had not died of cancer? He loved her, and she was good for him and his career. What if he had not quit the qualified psychotherapist he had found but stayed to work through his problems? What if?

25. MRS. KOESTLER AND MRS. ZWEIG:

DEVOTED WIVES

A survey of the United States from 1980 to 1987 documented about one hundred couples in which one or both committed suicide. Two-thirds of these cases involved mercy killings followed by suicide, while one-third were double suicides. In the typical double suicide, the wife or both partners were ill, and the husband initiated the plan. The couple often left evidence indicating that they felt exhausted and hopeless, and that they feared parting or being institutionalized.

For double suicides (rather than mercy killings), the research suggests the role of a domineering and dominating husband who decides that both partners must commit suicide. Insight into double suicide may be obtained from the biographies of two famous double suicides.

Charlotte Altman And Stefan Zweig

Stefan Zweig's family was upper middle class, Jewish and Viennese. Successful industrialists, bankers, and professional men were among his relatives. Stefan's father had established a large successful weaving mill in Czechoslovakia. His mother was from Italy and also Jewish.

Stefan was born the second and last child on November 28, 1881. As a child, he wanted for nothing. He was spoiled by his family, relatives and servants, but also severely disciplined. He was less obedient than his older brother, given to temper tantrums and often in conflict with his mother.

His older brother was expected to go into the father's business and agreed to do so. This left Stefan free to pursue his own interests, and Stefan chose an academic life. After eight grim years in a Gymnasium (a rigorous version of an extended American high school), he attended the University of Vienna and very quickly found that his interests lay in the theater and literature. He had poems published when he was sixteen, and he was soon writing for some of the best periodicals in Vienna. Almost everything he wrote was published, his first book when he was nineteen.

Despite his success, Stefan did not think highly of his writing, and so he decided to translate famous foreign authors rather than concentrate on his original compositions. One of the first poets that Stefan translated was the Belgian Emile Verhaeren, and this early translation work prepared Stefan for the role he played in European literature, the interpreter and introducer of foreign writers and their work to German audiences.

In 1912, Friderike von Winternitz, who had been tremendously moved by Stefan's early poems, initiated a romantic relationship with Stefan. At the time Friderike was married and had a daughter. Jewish by birth, she had converted to her husband's Catholic religion. Her family was upper middle class, and her father-in-law had connections at the Austrian Court and in the Foreign Service. She wrote too (and continued to do so while married to Stefan). However, she abandoned her aspirations in order to raise her two daughters and smooth the way for Stefan's writing.

Their romance was slowed by Stefan's reluctance to get involved, his continual travel, and Friderike's marital bonds. Stefan felt that the relationship would worsen his depression, and he warned Friderike about his moods, his unstable life and his lack of plans for the future. Friderike left her husband and set up a home for Stefan and herself in 1914. Stefan gave up an affair with a French woman and moved in with Friderike, though he seems to have felt no grand passion for her. After the

First World War Stefan and Friderike, now married, lived in their house in Salzburg, visited by the many friends and admirers.

The 1930s saw two changes in Stefan's life. First, he separated from Friderike and took up with his assistant, Charlotte Altman. Second, the growing anti-semitism in Germany and Austria affected him profoundly. Unlike many Jews in those nations, Stefan accurately forecast the outcome. He knew that he had to escape, and so he began to spend longer amounts of time outside of Austria and eventually moved to England in 1938 after the Germany occupation of Austria.

Charlotte Altman became his secretary in 1933. As with Friderike, he seemed hardly to notice Lotte's devotion to him. He slipped into an involvement with her as unwittingly as he had with Friderike. The struggle between the two women for Stefan's love lasted three years. At times it seemed as if he might stay with Friderike, but Stefan identified the stress he was under with Friderike. Lotte promised a more peaceful life. Friderike remained friends with Stefan and continued to worry about his state of mind and to try to get him through difficult periods. Stefan helped Friderike escape from France to the United States, and Friderike sent him letters and books to Brazil which were important since he felt isolated and alone there.

Lotte was physically frail and suffered from asthma. Stefan's biographers suggest that his sexual relationship with her was probably unsatisfactory. Friends of Stefan remarked that one hardly noticed Lotte. She seemed non-existent. Certainly Stefan's biographers have little to say of her. Yet her passionate devotion to Stefan is clear in her decision to commit suicide with him.

Stefan and Lotte bought a house in Bath, England, where Stefan managed to continue his writing. After his divorce from Friderike, he and Lotte married in September 1939, three days after Chamberlain's declaration of war with Germany. Stefan was fifty-seven, Lotte thirty-one.

Stefan was convinced that England would fall to Hitler. By June of 1940, Denmark and Norway had fallen, followed by Belgium, the Netherlands and France. Stefan received invitations to lecture in the United States and South America, and he took this opportunity to escape from what he saw as the certain defeat of England. Stefan and Lotte went first to the United States and then to Brazil.

He and Lotte leased a house outside of Rio in Petropolis where he completed his autobiography and wrote his last works of fiction. His reception in Brazil was cool, in contrast to the adulation on his tours there in the 1930s and, once they were installed in their home, few friends visited. Stefan had spent most of life entertaining friends and visiting acquaintances all over Europe. Though he had complained of never having time to himself for his work, he now had all the time he needed but felt acutely isolated. The solace he had sought oppressed him.

He went to Rio for the Carnival, but on Shrove Tuesday (February 17) the news arrived of the fall of Singapore to the Japanese. Stefan immediately left with Lotte for Petropolis. The decision was made. Stefan spent the rest of the week writing letters and making final arrangements. He called friends, and on Saturday evening invited a neighboring couple to dinner. On Sunday afternoon, he and Lotte both took massive doses of veronal and died.

Stefan's life was relatively easy compared to others living through the same era. He knew this, and it caused him guilt. His writing came easy, he was always wealthy, and he escaped from the terrible persecution and extermination of the Jews who stayed in Nazi-controlled Europe.

According to his biographers, Stefan was incapable

of forming close relationships. Stefan seemed closer to Friderike the further he was away from her. Perhaps Stefan feared the demands that would be made on him by close relationships? His life-style of frequently going off by himself to visit friends abroad served to preserve his relationship with her. Indeed, the same might be said of all of his friendships, which seemed to flourish better by letter than face-to-face.

The young Stefan was described as a melancholy introvert. He had periods of deep depression from an early age. His depressions may have been made worse by the persecution of his people by the Nazis and the banning and destruction of his works. He feared that the Nazis would eventually catch up with him and exterminate him no matter where he fled. In letter to a friend, he confided that the Nazis would never find him alive.

In a letter in 1931, he wrote that he feared being ill, growing old or growing bitter. For Stefan, sixty was the end of life. The difficulty he had in writing in the 1940s also terrified him.

Stefan had never attempted suicide prior to his death, but he had twice tried to persuade Friderike to join him in death. She had always talked him out it, and he had dealt with his depressions by traveling. Suicide was a prominent theme in his writing. Rather than allow his characters to endure humiliation from external forces in the society or from mental and physical deterioration, he had them escape, often by suicide.

His suicide note spoke only of his lack of desire to begin completely afresh in his sixtieth year. He spoke of being exhausted by long years of homeless wandering and his desire to avoid any future humiliation from loss of freedom and an inability to continue his intellectual work.

It remains a puzzle why Lotte died with him. He most certainly urged her to do so. But we learn so little about her from his biographers that we do not know why she submitted to such a suggestion. Clearly, Friderike did not and would not have died with him. Friderike was a writer too, had two children by her first husband and had learnt to live apart from Stefan since he traveled so extensively during their marriage. After the war, Friderike became an academic, one of the scholarly experts on Stefan Zweig.

Lotte died with Stefan; Friderike built a career on him!

Cynthia Jeffries And Arthur Koestler

Arthur Koestler was born on September 5, 1905, in Budapest, the only child of Henrik and Adela Koestler. The first trauma for Arthur was an unexpected and unexplained tonsillectomy without anesthesia in 1910. Because of his father's poor business sense and his mother's dislike of Hungary, the family moved to Vienna in 1914 amidst much conflict between his parents.

Shy and insecure, Koestler studied science and engineering, but he became involved in a Zionist dueling fraternity at a polytechnic college in Vienna. The three years he spent in this group were very happy and began his involvement in politics. He became a follower of Vladimir Jabotinsky, burned his matriculation papers and left for Palestine in 1926. After a hard period of adjustment there, he obtained a job as Middle East correspondent for a German publishing company.

In 1929, disillusioned with Palestine, he returned to Europe where he continued to work as a newspaper correspondent. He joined the German Communist Party in 1931 and lost his job as a result. He traveled to Russia to report on events there and returned to Paris to write, though the Communist Party disapproved of many of his articles and books and greatly restricted his freedom. He married Dorothy Asher but separated a few months later. (They were divorced in 1950.)

He made three trips to Spain during the Civil War and was arrested and imprisoned for three months by Franco's Nationalists as a spy. He was sentenced to death but freed after British protests. Disillusioned now with Communism, he resigned from the Communist Party. He was detained and imprisoned in both England and France but, after the publication of Darkness at Noon, was released. He worked for the Ministry of Information in England during the war.

After the war, the cause of Zionism again captured his attention, and he traveled there and both reported on events and wrote novels around his experiences. In 1950 he married Mamaine Paget, but she separated from him in 1951 and died in 1954 soon after their divorce. His third and final marriage was to Cynthia Jeffries in 1965, his secretary since 1950.

He settled in England in 1952, became a British citizen, and continued to work for and write about political issues. His writings, including both novels, essays, and biographies, always explored the important social issues of the times, and his work has been compared to George Orwell's in its impact on the times.

Cynthia Jeffries was twenty-two when she started working for Koestler. She was from South Africa and had gone to Paris with the aim of working for a writer. There had been stress in her life — her father committed suicide when she was thirteen and there was a brief, unsuccessful marriage. From the time that she joined him, her life was rarely distinct from his.

One of the causes for which Koestler worked was euthanasia. As he grew older, he developed Parkinson's disease and then leukemia. When the effects of these illnesses worsened, he decided to commit suicide, and Cynthia decided that she could not live without him.

Interestingly, all of his wives remained in some way attached and, for some, devoted to and dependent on him. Dorothy Asher helped free Koestler from prison in Spain. Mamaine Paget, who suffered from his drunken rages, wrote that she would do anything, even leave him, if it were necessary to help him fulfil his destiny.

Cynthia went further. On March 3, 1983, she committed suicide with him in their London home.

There was some outcry after the double suicide of the Koestlers. Koestler had treated Cynthia abominably. She had to be on duty to serve Arthur twenty-four hours a day, and she had to be perfect in everything she did. She was secretary, lover, wife, nurse, housekeeper, cook, mother, daughter and inseparable companion. Arthur criticized Cynthia's cooking early in their relationship and sent her to cooking school to improve. In the 1970s, Arthur became more dependent on Cynthia, especially after he lost his driving license for drunk driving and then as he developed Parkinson's disease and leukemia. He became Cynthia's prisoner, and she seemed more relaxed and teased Arthur more.

Cynthia was in good health, energetic and able. She had a home, many friends and financial security. But Cynthia had come to live entirely for Arthur and through him. As she added to Arthur's suicide note, "I cannot face life without Arthur."

It is common for those physically abused by others to feel that they deserve the abuse and for them to become dependent upon and attached to their abusers. Cynthia was not physically abused, but the psychological abuse may have created a similarly strong dependency upon Arthur. As Arthur sickened, Cynthia's attachment to him became less pathological but no less intense. His sickness, by making him more dependent upon her, gave her a little more power. But he obviously made no effort to prepare her for his death by encouraging her to have interests outside of his life or by encouraging her independence.

A myth in our society is that women die for love

while men die for glory. This myth, acting as a culturally-shared assumption, may influence the suicidal choices of women, and it is evident that such a culturally-shaped attitude may have played a role in the decisions of Lotte Zweig and Cynthia Koestler to commit suicide with their husbands.

In fact, though the deaths of Charlotte Zweig and Cynthia Koestler were technically suicides, their deaths have the quality of murder, murder by self-centered, power-seeking husbands who gave little or no thought for their wives' quality of life.

26. ULRIKE MEINHOF:

A GERMAN TERRORIST

Ulrike Meinhof was one of the leading terrorists in the 1970s in West Germany who committed numerous bank robberies, assassinations and bomb attacks. She was eventually captured, but she committed suicide in prison before sentencing.

Meinhof was born October 7, 1934, in Oldenburg, and she experienced, of course, the violence of the Second World War. Her father, a museum director, died of cancer during the war when she was six years old. Her mother was an art teacher, and Meinhof attended a Roman Catholic parochial school. Her mother soon died too, and Meinhof was reared by a foster parent, Professor Renate Riemeck, who encouraged her academic studies and guided her toward a liberal political viewpoint.

Meinhof was a good student, and went to the University of Munich. While there, she got involved with the ban-the-bomb movement, one of the leaders of which was her foster-father. She also met Klaus Roehl who was the publisher of the magazine Konkret in Hamburg which had become the voice of the left-wing student movement. She started to write for the magazine, became its editor-in-chief and married Roehl. A year later she gave birth to twins. She became a celebrity as the outstanding, left-wing, glamorous writer and television polemicist of the 1960s. Meinhof and Roehl had also traveled to East Germany and secured Communist funds to support the magazine, but the Communist Party gave them free rein over the contents of the magazine which resembled Playboy more than Pravda. In 1965, Meinhof developed a brain tumor, and a clamp had to be inserted into her brain to ease the pressure.

Meinhof began to tire of the words of protest, but she was still opposed to violence. Her young brother-in-law once pulled out a revolver in the woods and shot it, producing a hysterical fit in Meinhof and a mild nervous breakdown. She did not talk to this brother-in-law for a year. As her dissatisfaction with her way of life grew, she divorced Roehl and moved from Hamburg to West Berlin with her daughters.

There, she joined the Ausser Parlamentarische Opposition (Extraparliamentary Opposition or APO), led by Rudi Dutschke (Red Rudy). The APO was anti-American, anti-Vietnam War, anti-imperialist, and anti-establishment. When members of the group fire-bombed two warehouses in April, 1968, as a protest against the Vietnam War, Meinhof visited them in prison and was impressed by them, especially Andreas Baader, born in May 1943. Baader was a happy-go-lucky type with a criminal history, but he was able to move the group from theory into action. Together with Meinhof, they gradually assumed the leadership of the group which was named after them, the Baader-Meinhof Gang.

Of the original twenty-two members, ten were women, and eight of the next twenty members were women. Baader was sentenced to three years for the fire-bombings but was released after serving nine months, pending final sentencing. He failed to return to the courts and began an underground existence.

Meinhof continued to write and lecture, and her first "violent" act was to take some members of the gang and vandalize her ex-husband's house. They destroyed the furnishings, defaced the walls and urinated on the bed.

Baader was captured in April 1970, but Meinhof and gang members used tear-gas and guns to attack the guards who were transporting Baader and succeeded in freeing him. Two guards and a librarian were injured, but lived. Two weeks later, Meinhof, Baader and a few other members went to Jordan to train at an al-Fatah Palestinian training camp. Returning to Germany, the wave of terror began in earnest — eighty bombings and arson assaults in West Berlin alone in 1970, including three simultaneous bank robberies on September 29, 1970. A week later, all three banks were bombed. The radical left, including the Baader-Meinhof Gang, was responsible for 555 acts of terrorism in 1971. In one week in May 1972, fifteen bombs exploded in West Germany, damaging the headquarters of the U.S. Fifth Army, the Augsburg Police Headquarters and the Munich Criminal Investigation Office. The gang was the most successful terrorist group in Europe after the Irish Republican Army in Northern Ireland.

Baader was captured on June 1, and Meinhof on June 15 after a "friend" gave her away to the authorities. Meinhof was kept in solitary confinement, with the lights permanently on, despite protests by her lawyers that this was cruel and inhumane treatment. She led three hunger strikes, for a month beginning January 1973, for seven weeks beginning May and for five months beginning September 1974, during which one of the prisoners died despite forced feeding.

The major trial began in June 1975, despite protests over the fact the original defense attorneys had been barred from the court and the new attorneys had no time to prepare. When the trial began, the prisoners refused to participate and were tried in absentia.

The imprisonment and hunger strikes had weakened all of them. Meinhof was forgetful and had trouble articulating, concentrating and even perceiving clearly. She felt weak and had headaches, and she had lost twenty-eight pounds. Finally, on May 8, 1976, while the other members of the group were exercising, she hung herself with a white prison towel from the bars of her cell.

27. CHARLOTTE PERKINS GILMAN:

AN EARLY FEMINIST

Charlotte Gilman was a leading feminist of the late 19th and early 20th Centuries who committed suicide in old age when dying of cancer. She was born as Charlotte Perkins on July 3, 1860, in Hartford, Connecticut. Her father, Frederick Perkins, was a Beecher, probably the most famous family in America. He was not as successful as the typical Beecher, failing to graduate from Yale University and working as a librarian in addition to writing. He married a distant cousin, Mary Westcott, also with English roots, and they had three children, Thomas who died after a month, another Thomas and finally Charlotte. After Charlotte's birth, his wife was told that she might die if she had another child, whereupon Frederick left the home. Mary had a fourth child in 1866 (after a visit from Frederick) who died after eight months. From 1863 to 1873, Mary and her two children stayed with assorted relatives or in rented rooms, mostly in New England. Mary divorced Frederick in 1873, whereupon the Beechers turned against her.

Frederick did not abandon his family. He visited and provided some financial support, but he was a distant figure for Charlotte. She missed him and was angry at him, but rarely permitted that anger to appear. Matters were made worse by the decision of her mother to withhold affection from her children so that they would suffer less from rejection later in life! Charlotte's older brother was rather mean to her, though they did become somewhat dependent on each other and had some good times together. Thomas tried various jobs in his life, failing at most, and his family was supported in part by Charlotte.

Charlotte first made a collection of her literary pieces when she was ten, but her mother disliked Charlotte engaging in "fantasy" and discouraged her from reading and from having friends. Luckily, after a couple of years, Charlotte disobeyed her mother. She did decide, however, to live with her mother and follow most of her rules until she was twenty-one. From age sixteen to twenty-one, Charlotte laid out a program for self-improvement for herself, including exercise. She had only four years of schooling, and none after the age of fifteen. She took care of her ailing mother and was often depressed and weary. Still, she did have friends with whom she played games almost every evening, and she visited relatives. She painted (and sold a little of her work), gave private lessons and taught art classes. She studied at the Rhode Island School of Design (against her mother's wishes) and took correspondence courses at home on a variety of academic subjects. She developed a close friendship with Martha Luther whom she met when she was seventeen which lasted until Martha married four years later, a loss which affected Charlotte deeply.

In 1882, Charlotte met Walter Stetson, a young artist born in March 1858. By the time Charlotte met him, he was well-respected, had some works accepted at exhibitions, and had attracted a few patrons. He proposed marriage after three weeks, but Charlotte hesitated for two years. Walter wanted a pure and loving traditional wife and, with much forboding and anxiety, Charlotte finally married him in May 1884. A daughter, Katharine, was born in March 1885.

Charlotte lived a split life with Walter. At home she was deeply depressed and could barely function as wife or mother. At the same time, she managed to function much better away from home. In 1885, she took a break away from her family with friends in Pasadena where she painted and wrote a play with her friend, Grace

Channing, whom she had met in her teens in Providence. Back home, her depression returned. Yet, she visited the gym and wrote a suffrage column for a local weekly newspaper in Providence. She also published several poems in the Woman's Journal.

In 1887, she went into treatment in Philadelphia with Dr. Silas Mitchell who tried to give women a time-out from their stressful lives, but who wanted them to return to and enjoy their traditional role. Charlotte returned to Walter and felt even worse than before. She came close to having a nervous breakdown. She and Walter decided to part and, after a year, Charlotte left (in September 1888) with her child for Pasadena.

In her two years in Pasadena, Charlotte earned money by giving art lessons, tutoring, lecturing and selling her writing. In the first year, she wrote 33 articles and 23 poems. She joined a theater group as actor and interior designer. She also began to be known as a social critic.

Walter visited in late 1889, and a relationship developed between him and Grace. Grace left to be with Walter on the East Coast in the fall of 1890, and she eventually married him in 1894. Charlotte missed Grace tremendously, but she sent her daughter to live with Grace and Walter in May 1894.

Charlotte moved to Oakland in 1891, remaining in the area until 1895. During this period, her reputation as a writer and lecturer grew. She was known as a socialist and a feminist. Most of her lectures became journal articles and provided material for her books, and by the end of her life she had lectured on more than two hundred topics. While in Oakland, she briefly ran a journal Impress, published her first book of poems, and became active in a number of organizations. In her personal life she met (in May 1891) and perhaps became lovers with a woman, Adeline Knapp, a relationship which ended acrimoniously in early 1893. In 1891, her ailing mother came to live with Charlotte and soon developed cancer, and Charlotte was often exhausted with the demands made on her by personal and professional commitments. Charlotte filed for divorce in 1892 and was granted it in 1894, an event which made headline news. Her mother died in March 1893, but Charlotte's father had visited several times during her stay in Oakland and now kept in touch with his daughter, sometimes helping her out with money.

In 1895, at the age of thirty-five, Charlotte was now truly alone and independent. For the next five years, until her marriage in 1900, she traveled across America and abroad, lecturing and writing. Her activity was interrupted by frequent depressive spells, but she learned to endure these periods knowing that her spirits would eventually revive.

Her first book on society's problems, Women and Economics, was published in 1898 to great acclaim. She followed this with a series of volumes: Concerning Children, The Home, Human Work, The Man-Made World, and His Religion and Hers. Although by modern standards, there are problems with her writing (for example, she was rather racist), her works were innovative and provocative, and her radical views received widespread attention. For seven years, from 1909 to 1916, she wrote and published a monthly magazine Forerunner, each issue with 32 pages, with the total run equivalent to 28 books. Over her lifetime, she also wrote at least 186 pieces of fiction and 490 poems. Her fiction consisted both of realistic stories of women's lives and utopian visions.

In 1897, she visited a first-cousin, Houghton Gilman, born in 1867, whom she had known since childhood, a moderately successful lawyer in New York City, and they fell in love and decided to marry. The marriage took place in June 1900, and their relationship was stable and happy. Houghton appreciated the needs of his wife and her desire for a career and did all he could to facilitate it. They decided to not have children for fear of possible defects in their offspring due to their close genetic relationship.

As her life progressed, her depressions came less often, but her standing declined. After the First World War, her ideas were rather dated. Her books sold less well, and her lectures were less in demand. Charlotte became somewhat bitter in her final years about the relative indifference with which her ideas were met. Although she earned a reasonable income, she never was financially comfortable, and Houghton earned too little from his legal work to make much difference.

Her relationship with her daughter grew closer, though they never discussed their feelings about the separation and Katharine remained angry at her mother's action. After Katharine married, Charlotte and Houghton often helped out financially (as they did for Charlotte's brother too).

Charlotte and Houghton lived in New York City from 1900 to 1922, and then they moved to a home they inherited which they shared with Houghton's brother and his wife despite much friction between the two couples.

In 1932, Charlotte found out that she had inoperable and terminal breast cancer. Though she worried about how Houghton would live after her death, he died unexpectedly of a cerebral hemorrhage on May 4, 1934. She sold her share of the house to her brother-in-law and moved to Pasadena to be near her daughter. She rented a room and continued to busy herself with her causes, and she enjoyed being a grandmother. She gave lectures and, since she could persuade no one to write her biography, worked on her autobiography. She tried x-ray treatments for the cancer in 1934, but thereafter decided to let it take its course. She reluctantly took morphine for the pain in 1935 and finally informed

Katharine about the illness in March 1935. Katharine insisted that her mother come and live with her, and Grace managed to find enough money to visit Charlotte for her final weeks.

By August 1935, Charlotte had revised her autobiography and finished the proofreading. Many years earlier, in the Forerunner, Charlotte had expressed her disapproval of suicide except when people are "beyond usefulness." Just prior to her death she was asked to contribute an article on euthanasia (which was published posthumously), in which she developed these ideas.

In August 1935, Charlotte told her family of her plans, and on August 17, 1935, she killed herself by inhaling chloroform, a methods she had described in the Forerunner article in 1912 as in "good taste."

Charlotte Gilman survived a nervous breakdown during her first marriage and periodic depressions throughout her life, but she seems to have not been seriously suicidal until her progressive cancer in old age. Having nursed her mother through a death from cancer, she decided, probably rationally, that a premature death was a sensible choice.

28. ABBIE HOFFMAN:

HIPPIE AND YIPPIE

Abbie's ancestors were Russian Jews, named Shapoznikoff, from an area near Kiev ("The Pale"). Abbie's father arrived in the United States in 1906 at the age of one, getting the name Hoffman from an uncle who had obtained papers in that name. John Hoffman worked in his uncle's drugstore, studied at night for a degree in pharmacy and started a wholesale distributorship of medical supplies. Abbie's mother was born in Clinton, Massachusetts, near Worcester; her father was a wrecker, and her mother worked in a sweatshop. She worked as a secretary, met John at a bowling alley and married him in 1935.

Abbie was born on November 30, 1936; a younger brother was born in 1939 and sister in 1941. Abbie liked to be the center of attention (and had asthma attacks when not), and was healthy, active and mischievous. (At the age of thirteen, the police accused him of changing around the license plates of neighborhood cars.) Jews were a tiny minority in Worcester, and Abbie's parents were not strict. They did not participate in the larger Jewish community, and Abbie grew up feeling "American" and was never defensive about his Jewish identity. John Hoffman was a civic booster for Worcester, and had high standing in Worcester community. He died in 1974, shortly after Abbie went underground, feeling that his son had let him down.

Abbie liked sports, both playing and watching, and he and his father supported the Boston Red Sox and the Holy Cross College teams. He excelled at tennis and was a champion at yo-yo tricks. Abbie showed no interest in politics or social issues. In his teenage years, perhaps in rebellion, Abbie hung out with the local Irish and Italian youths, playing pool and poker and dating gentile girls. Nevertheless, he got good grades at school and voraciously read the books he borrowed from the public library. He also helped out his father in his business and was a good salesman. In June, 1953, a tornado hit the Worcester area, and Abbie worked through the night ordering medical supplies and distributing them to the Red Cross and local authorities.

As a sophomore, he wrote a paper defending atheism, had an argument with the teacher about it, and hit the teacher when he called Abbie a communist bastard. He was suspended, but enrolled at the Worcester Academy, a private boarding school. He graduated in June 1995, and went to Brandeis University.

In 1955, Brandeis University, founded by Jews, was seven years old. It had attracted many left-wing professors who had escaped Joseph McCarthy's witch hunts, partly because McCarthy did not want to appear to be anti-semitic. Abbie initially planned to become a physician, but a course from Abraham Maslow, a leading humanistic psychologist, led Abbie to major in psychology. Maslow became an idol for Abbie.

At Brandeis, Abbie identified with the bohemian crowd, but did not abandon his love of sports and gambling. He also earned eighty dollars a week selling sandwiches to the other students at night in the dormitories. Abbie attended lectures from Martin Luther King, Dorothy Day and Saul Alinsky. But Maslow remained Abbie's hero, and Abbie set out to become self-actualized. Only later did he focus on the political implications of Maslow's ideas.

Abbie next studied psychology for a year at the University of California at Berkeley, and he continued his undergraduate life-style — studying, shooting pool, and operating a travel club. However, Abbie's year there did get him involved in political issues (a fight over ROTC on campus, protests against the execution of Caryl Chessman, and a local hearing by the House Committee on Un-American Activities [HUAC]).

Abbie's girlfriend, Sheila Karklin, visited him at Berkeley and got pregnant. They married in the summer of 1960, eventually having two children together. He got a job as a staff psychologist at Worcester State Hospital (though he did not have a master's degree), but soon began to get involved in activism. The local ACLU chapter hired him to travel around Massachusetts with a film about the HUAC defending the anti-HUAC position. After trying to run a movie theater for "good movies", Abbie got a job in sales for a pharmaceutical company, and helped in H. Stuart Hughes's campaign for the United States Senate.

Abbie became friendly with a local priest, Father Bernard Gilgun, and Abbie and Sheila were caught up by his activism. Abbie established regular Friday meetings attended by hundreds where speakers led discussions on social issues. Abbie and Sheila involved themselves in local civil rights activity (such as the local NAACP chapter). Sheila organized the first peace demonstrations, and Abbie started a newsletter, The Drum. Abbie was a whirlwind in the community, involving himself in everything, but he never stayed with any project. Abbie did not want power; he wanted action.

Abbie and Sheila supported the work of black activists in the South, raising money for them, and trying (unsuccessfully) to get the alternative delegation from Mississippi admitted to the Democratic convention in Atlantic City in 1964. In 1965, Abbie and Sheila went to the South to work with the freedom fighters. When he came back north, Abbie helped the southern blacks market and sell their locally-made products in retail outlets in the North. In 1966, he was fired from his job, and his marriage broke up. Abbie decided to move to New York City.

In New York, Abbie devoted himself to social causes, also writing about them which added to his growing reputation. Abbie quickly met and fell in love with a young woman, Anita, a graduate of Goucher College, with a master's degree in psychology, and they moved in together (and were married in 1967). Abbie also got involved in the hippie culture. He smoked marijuana and took acid, and he lived in the East Village with other hippies. Abbie then decided that he could turn the rebellion of the hippies in a political direction.

He began by developing a support network for the hippies — raising seed money for projects, running a newsletter, providing bail and legal aid, free food, free clothes, etc. Abbie also decided to develop the idea formulated by others of using theater in protests. To protest the traffic on St. Marks Place, Abbie and others transformed the place into a dance stage and pedestrian mall one evening. The next week they "planted" a tree in the road and danced. Abbie took free old clothes to Macy's and "gave them away" and, in one of his most famous exploits, in 1967 threw one dollar bills into the trading floor at the New York Stock Exchange from the visitors' balcony, with the result that the traders on the floor fought over the money.

Starting in 1967, Abbie became more involved in the effort to stop the war in Vietnam. Working with hippies, Abbie devised guerrilla theater. He led a group in a Loyalty Parade, with flowers and "LOVE" signs, and was attacked by the groups supporting the Johnson administration. His group received as much media attention as the "loyal" groups. In late 1967, as part of the protest in Washington, DC, against the war, Abbie led an "exorcism" of the Pentagon and tried to levitate it.

These exploits led up to the Democratic Convention in Chicago in 1968. Abbie and others organized themselves as "Yippies", nominated a pig for President, and planned a series of protests. However, the authoritarian mayor of Chicago, Richard Daley, refused to issue permits for parades or for the protesters to sleep in the parks. He also called out the National Guard and had them and the Chicago police officers attack and beat the protesters. Many, including Abbie, were arrested. Although, of course, many Americans approved of the acts of the authorities in Chicago, others were outraged. The brutality of the authorities, which the Democratic candidate for President, Hubert Humphrey, supported, contributed to Humphrey's defeat in the election. Abbie, having exposed the brutality of the authorities, considered the events a great victory for the movement.

It was here, in the midst of confrontations with other protesters and the authorities, that Abbie was, for the first time, occasionally out-of-control and in a manic phase. It was also now that the police, including the FBI, began their continuous surveillance of Abbie. They interrogated him a number of times, tapped his telephone calls and broke into his offices.

Back in New York, Abbie found it hard to keep the movement going. Some of his associates dropped out to start rural communes; others turned to environmental issues. Abbie's book, "Revolution For The Hell Of It," published in 1968 kept Abbie in the spotlight. MGM bought the movie rights (though the movie was never made), and Abbie gave the money ($25,000) to the Black Panther bail fund.

One of Abbie's achievements was to end the public hearings of the HUAC. The committee ordered Abbie to Washington, DC, for questioning. Abbie dressed himself in a shirt made out of the American flag. The police tried to arrest him on the Capitol steps but tore the shirt, all of which was captured by television. The committee suspended hearings, tried to resume them a month later, but never again organized a public hearing.

At Woodstock, Abbie failed to organize any Yippie

events, but he saw that the volunteer effort needed organizing and took over. For example, he helped organize a medical station and printed survival bulletins. On his return to New York, he wrote Woodstock Nation.

On March 20, 1969, Abbie along with seven others, were indicted in a Chicago federal court for their "crimes" during the Democratic convention. Abbie took the lead in creating the public image for the group, though the judge, Julius Hoffman, was so inept that he made it easy for the defendants. For example, when the Black Panther, Bobbie Seale, insisted on defending himself, the judge ordered Seale bound and gagged in court, eventually separating his trial from that of the others. However, Abbie and the rest of the Chicago Seven, also heckled and pulled pranks on the judge, goading him until he lost control. The trial began in late September, 1969, and the jury began its deliberations on February 14, 1970. After four days they were deadlocked, but the judge forced decisions from them. The judge sentenced the defendants to five years in prison and five thousand dollar fines. They spent two weeks in jail before their appeals led to their release. In 1972, the court of appeals threw out most of the contempt-of-court citations, and later overturned all of the convictions. In 1973, a reduced number of contempt charges were upheld and the defendants sentenced to the time already served.

Abbie was now in demand for public talks at a thousand dollars a time, a celebrity, a symbol of the polarized society, loathed by many and extolled by others. The FBI followed him everywhere, planted hostile stories in the press and tried to prevent his speaking engagements. The capitalists tried to take him over — to hire him as a youth consultant for their marketing departments or to make Abbie Hoffman dolls. He refused.

However, it proved to be difficult for Abbie to find a focus, and in early 1970 he and Anita were demoralized and talked of going into exile to Cuba. Nixon's invasion of Cambodia in April and the murder of Kent State University students by the National Guard energized them. After the New York City police raided a gay bar in Greenwich Village in June 1969 which led to violent protests by the gay community, gay causes were a growing concern, and the feminist movement was also growing. Abbie wrote a book entitled Steal This Book, which contained advice on how to get things for free, both legally and illegally. No publisher would accept it, and he was forced to publish it himself. 100,000 copies were sold in the first four months! Nevertheless Abbie began to feel unappreciated and put upon. He lacked a good support network, and he had organized no business. He had no staff, no press agent and little money. He loved fame, while despising himself for loving it. He was good at public theater, but had no desire to go into the legitimate theater. Working in advertising or consultancy would have violated his principles, and public office held no charm. Anita, tired of her identity as Abbie's wife, went to live in Long Island, though Abbie visited and stayed with her and their child often. It was on Long Island that Abbie began using cocaine, and that gave him the idea to make some money with a cocaine deal.

Abbie made no secret about his plans, and the arrangements were amateurish. He was arrested during the deal. As his friends and lawyers tried to work on his behalf, raising funds and trying to control the damage to Abbie's reputation, Abbie decided to jump bail and go underground. In February, 1974, after a speech in Atlanta, he disappeared. His support network helped him, and the danger was not that the police would find him, but rather that Abbie himself might be so reckless that he would give away his identity.

In the summer of 1974, he went to Mexico and fell in love with Johanna Lawrenson. He considered going to Israel, gave an interview to Top Value Television (shown on Public Television in May, 1975), and was interviewed for the Playboy issue of May, 1976. As the date for this issue grew closer, Abbie had his second manic episode since going underground. He thought that his friends had betrayed him, and he fled to Montreal where he ran up huge bills at the hotel by calling people in America. He developed grandiose plans, was very paranoid, and walked around carrying a hunting knife. A friend in Montreal introduced him to a psychiatrist who was opposed to medication, and so Abbie did not get the medication necessary to calm him down. Eventually, Johanna got him back to America and settled down on one of the Thousand Islands in the St. Lawrence Seaway.

Abbie passed himself off as Barry Freed, a free-lance writer, and at first he finished his autobiography for publication. He and Johanna traveled to Europe, Mexico and Los Angeles, and Abbie threw a party for himself at the Felt Forum at Madison Square Garden. In 1980, he was examined by a psychiatrist in Los Angeles who diagnosed Abbie as having a bipolar affective disorder and prescribed lithium. Thereafter, Abbie was much more stable psychologically, as long as he took the medication. However, since it upset his stomach, he often refused to take it which brought back his manic and depressive moods.

He quickly became involved in a community effort to prevent the St. Lawrence Seaway from being kept open all year. Starting in 1978, Abbie helped organize the groups, and this time he attended to all of the tasks that need to be done to accomplish such a goal. He got people involved, set up a sound financial basis, co-opted all kinds of groups even though they might disagree on other issues, lobbied the right people, etc, and he did this behind the scenes since it was still dangerous for Abbie/Barry to become the center of media attention.

Toward the end of 1980, Abbie began to consider surrendering to the police and, once the decision was made, he turned it into a media event. Barbara Walters was given the story, and she announced it on ABC's national news on September 3, 1980. He pleaded guilty to a lesser charge and was scheduled for sentencing in April 1981. He was sentenced to three years in prison — he served two months in maximum security and ten months in a New York City drug rehabilitation program.

He was quite active in prison (for example, teaching English to the Spanish-speaking prisoners) and at the center (where he worked as a counselor). After parole, however, Abbie again had difficulty finding a cause on which to focus his energies. A project to combine the myriad community groups to protect the Great Lakes failed but, in December 1982, Abbie was given the opportunity to help prevent a pumping station being built to siphon off water from the Delaware River to cool a nuclear power plant. In a few days, he devised a strategy to halt the impending construction, and again he organized the local groups to defeat the project — which they did in a referendum in May, 1983. Abbie stopped taking his lithium during this period of activity, and his mania soon returned. He became paranoid and violent, and his friends could not calm him down. He resigned from the local group (and the St. Lawrence Seaway group too), returned to New York, where his mania crested in April, to be followed by a severe depression. He attempted suicide with 75 Restorils, but survived after being taken to Bellevue Hospital.

This experience motivated him to work on bipolar affective disorder. He attended psychiatric conferences and started self-help groups for people like himself. He continued to take his lithium for two years, but in 1985 he switched to self-medication, using Valium to neutralize his mania and antidepressants for the depressions. However, on this regimen, he still suffered from mood swings, though they were not as severe as before.

Abbie spent 1984 to 1989 doing what he had tried to do earlier in his life, foment a youth rebellion, giving some sixty speeches a year. He tried to start a National Student Organization. Abbie himself was unacceptable to many of the students involved, and he worked for this goal through a group of students at Rutgers University who respected him. However, the resulting organization did not achieve much — there were no galvanizing issues to motivate the students.

He got involved with the Sandinistas in Nicaragua, making five trips there. He was arrested with Amy Carter (President Carter's daughter) at the University of Massachusetts in Amherst protesting CIA recruiters on campus. At this trial, Abbie worked with the system and defended his group successfully — the jury acquitted them.

In 1987, he returned to Pennsylvania to fight the pumping station project again, but this time his group lost. He decided to stay in the area. On June 16, 1988, he was driving to Newark airport to hand-deliver an article to Playboy on the possibility that President Reagan had struck an arms-for-hostages deal with Iran, when his careless driving led to a severe crash in which he lost consciousness. He refused treatment, made his flight to Chicago in order to deliver his article only to find out that Playboy objected to some of it. They planned to print only the part that had adequate documentation. He collapsed after returning to New York and was treated for a broken leg, broken rib, punctured kidney and two broken fingers!

The injuries healed slowly, and the pain was quite bad. He also fell into the severest depression since his suicide attempt six years earlier. Although he was planning more college speeches and was exploring the possibility of an academic teaching position, the depression worsened. By February, 1989, he felt he was losing control. He tried Prozac, but it did not seem to help. On April 12, Johanna and other friends telephoned his apartment but could get no answer. They called his landlord who found Abbie dead. He had taken about 150 phenobarbitals and washed them down with alcohol. His first attempt failed because he forget the alcohol. This time, he remembered.

Abbie Hoffman, who had spent his adult life using the media to promote his causes, died a very private death.

29. CLEOPATRA:

SUCCESSFUL RULER OF EGYPT

Cleopatra has received a "bad press" because most of the presumed facts of Cleopatra's life are distortions introduced by those who have written about her. Cleopatra appears to have been a faithful wife and lover and a pretty good ruler of her kingdom.

Cleopatra VII was born in 69 BC in Egypt, the third child of Ptolemy XII. The dynasty was founded by a Macedonian general who became the ruler of Egypt after the death of Alexander the Great in 323 BC. Since the Egyptian royal family favored incestuous marriage, Cleopatra was mainly of Greek descent.

The Egyptian empire had shrunk over the years so that it now consisted of only Egypt itself. The Romans had taken over many of Egypt's former territories, and the threat of annexation by Rome was real. Ptolemy XII offered Rome his help in exchange for protection from his enemies. In 59 BC Julius Caesar and Pompey (who together ruled Rome with Crassus) declared publicly that Ptolemy had the right to his throne and charged him 6,000 talents for this (about the size of the Egypt's annual revenue). Two years later, his subjects led protests against him, and he fled to Rome, possibly taking his twelve year-old daughter, Cleopatra, with him.

While he was in Rome, his first-born, a daughter, Cleopatra VI Tryphaena, usurped his throne. Ptolemy borrowed another 10,000 talents to pay for Roman soldiers but, by the time they returned to Egypt, Cleopatra VI had been killed by Ptolemy's supporters and his second-born, also a daughter, Berenice, had seized the throne. The Romans, including a young officer, Mark Antony, defeated her forces and restored

Ptolemy, who quickly had Berenice executed. Ptolemy died in 51 BC, whereupon Cleopatra, aged eighteen, and her younger brother, Ptolemy aged ten, were declared joint heirs.

Cleopatra was not particularly beautiful, but she had a nice voice and "force of character." The first two years of her reign did not go well. The floods failed (leading to a poor harvest), and there was more civil unrest, especially because her people did not approve of her allegiance to Rome. She agreed to send troops to help the Romans in Syria, but her troops refused to go. The young Ptolemy had a regent, a eunuch named Pothinus, who was hostile to Cleopatra, and soon Pothinus issued edicts in Ptolemy's name alone, as if Cleopatra had been deposed.

When Caesar and Pompey began their Roman civil war, Pompey's son obtained Pothinus's help but when, after Pompey's defeat, Pompey went to Egypt, he was killed by the Egyptians as he tried to land. Four days later, Caesar reached Egypt. Caesar was angry that the Egyptians had killed a Roman and demanded the 6,000 talents (plus interest) that Rome was owed. The Egyptians rioted, and Caesar was forced to remain in the royal palace with Ptolemy and Pothinus. Cleopatra made her way into the place, despite Pothinus's attempts to keep her out, and became Caesar's lover. Caesar took her side in the power struggle, and arranged a marriage between Cleopatra and Ptolemy and decreed that they should rule jointly. It is unlikely that Ptolemy and Cleopatra ever consummated their marriage.

Cleopatra's younger sister, Arsinoe, left the palace and joined the rebel Egyptian forces, declaring herself Queen. Caesar had Pothinus executed on suspicion of being in league with Arsinoe and, when his reinforcements arrived, defeated the Egyptian forces. Afterwards Ptolemy was found drowned in the Nile, dragged down by the weight of his armor.

Caesar then married Cleopatra, still his lover, to another younger brother, Ptolemy XIV, then about twelve years old, and proclaimed them joint rulers of Egypt. Ptolemy had no powerful allies, and so Cleopatra now was the real ruler. Caesar left Egypt soon after this and, after more military triumphs, returned to Rome in 46 BC with Arsinoe as his prisoner.

Cleopatra visited Rome after Caesar had returned there, but she was kept well away from Caesar's wife. She had Caesar's son with her, Ptolemy Caesar (usually called Caesarion), and she stayed in Rome until Caesar's assassination in 44 BC. She returned to Egypt in July, and Ptolemy XIV died in September — his death remains a mystery. Cleopatra then named her son, Ptolemy XV Caesar, as her co-ruler.

Cleopatra was now in her mid-twenties, and for the next three years she devoted herself to governing Egypt. She did this very well, despite more flood failures which resulted in poor harvests.

Back in Rome, a civil war had broken out between Mark Antony and Octavius, and both appealed to Cleopatra for help. Cleopatra, like her predecessors, hedged her bets until she could be sure who would win. In 42 BC, Antony and Octavius split the Roman Empire between them, giving Mark Antony the eastern part. Antony, now forty and married for the third time, wanted to attack the Parthian empire and summoned Cleopatra to Tarsus in order to persuade her to help him in his campaign. They became lovers, and Cleopatra agreed to help him in return for his protection against her enemies, including the execution of Arsinoe. After a stay with Cleopatra in Alexandria, Mark Antony left for his territories. His wife died, and he married Octavius's sister, Octavia. Meanwhile, Cleopatra gave birth to twins by Antony, whom she named Alexander and Cleopatra Selene.

For the next three years, she returned to the task of governing Egypt and restoring its economy. She kept Egypt peaceful, learnt Egyptian, and observed the rites of Egyptian religion. By the end of the reign she had paid off the debts incurred by her father and by the demands of Caesar and Mark Antony. She appears to have made money from oil in territory near the Dead Sea and by leasing land around Jericho to King Herod of Judea.

In 37 BC, Mark Antony returned to his Parthian campaign and asked Cleopatra to help him. She bargained for land in what are now Lebanon, Syria, Jordan and southern Turkey. In return, Cleopatra built him a fleet. Resuming their political alliance, they also became lovers again. In May, 36 BC, Mark Antony departed for war, leaving Cleopatra pregnant (with Ptolemy Philadelphus). The war went badly, and he summoned Cleopatra again. She arrived in January, 35 BC, with money to pay his soldiers and winter clothing for the troops.

At this point Mark Antony made a momentous decision. He cast off Octavia (who had given him only daughters) and allied himself with Cleopatra (who had given him two sons), and he made Alexandria the center of his empire. Over the next six years until his death, Octavius, later the Emperor Augustus, cast Mark Antony as a traitor who had thrown in his lot with foreigners.

Mark Antony next had to deal with an uprising led by Sextus Pompey, a son of Pompey, who had seized towns in Asia Minor. After defeating Sextus, he granted the territories of his empire (and some yet to be conquered) to his three children. Thus, he was annexing these lands, not to Rome, but to the Egyptian empire. He made Caesarion, now thirteen, King of Kings and declared him the legitimate heir to Julius Caesar, a direct threat to Octavius. Mark Antony's plan was to leave the

Eastern Empire to the Ptolemys and take the Western Empire for himself.

From 33 BC on, preparations were made for the war. The battles in Greece went badly for Antony, and Cleopatra wanted to keep her hold over Antony by making her fleet indispensable. So Mark Antony chose to fight on sea rather than on land, and he lost. He and Cleopatra escaped to Alexandria with their ships which held the treasure which would allow them to fight on, while Octavius defeated the remaining resistance.

Cleopatra tried to escape with Caesarion to India, but Arabs attacked her ships in the Red Sea. In 30 BC Octavius returned to the east to deal with Mark Antony. Cleopatra offered to step down in favor of her children, but Octavius ignored her request. In August, 30 BC, Octavius had Alexandria besieged. Cleopatra locked herself in her monument with three attendants. Antony, believing that she had committed suicide, stabbed himself. Dying, he was hoisted into her monument where he died in her presence.

When Octavius's representative forced his way into Cleopatra's monument, she tried to kill herself, but was overpowered and taken prisoner. Octavius let it be known that he planned to take Cleopatra to Rome as his prisoner, possibly to encourage her to commit suicide. She got rid of the guard by giving him a letter to take to Octavius (which asked Octavius to bury her next to Mark Antony), and killed herself. It is not certain how she died — the only marks on her body were two tiny scratches on her arm. Perhaps she had some poison which she swallowed or perhaps she pricked herself with a poisoned pin?

Octavius had Caesarion executed, but he spared Mark Antony's three children. Little Cleopatra was married to Prince Juba of Numidia, and her two brothers led a quiet life with her there. Octavius then annexed Egypt.

Cleopatra probably had only two lovers in her life, Julius Caesar and Mark Antony, and she had four children with them. She was a good ruler and a shrewd politician. She died because she chose the wrong side in the Roman civil war.

30. REINALDO ARENAS:

A CUBAN WRITER WHO DIED OF AIDS

Arenas was born on July 16, 1943, in Holguín, Cuba. His mother, expecting to marry a young man, had slept with him and got pregnant, whereupon the man ran off, leaving her to bear her son. After living for a year with her prospective in-laws, she moved in with her parents, along with her many other single and abandoned sisters. As a fallen women, she would have had difficulty finding a husband, but, though depressed and sometimes suicidal, she decided to remain chaste for the rest of her life.

Arenas's grandfather was an alcoholic and physically abused his wife, but his grandmother was a strong woman who ran her large household efficiently. The grandfather farmed about a hundred acres (mostly for corn) and, though poor, the grandmother fed everyone and kept them healthy.

Homosexuality played a prominent role in Arenas's life, and his first homosexual memory was from the age of six when he saw a large group of men bathing naked in a river. The following day, he says, he discovered masturbation. Like his friends, most of his childhood sexual activity was with animals — hens, dogs, goats, pigs and horses. He even carved holes in soft-stemmed trees and fruits for sexual stimulation. His first heterosexual experience was with a cousin, but his first consummated act was with a male cousin when he was eight, and later an uncle use to sit Arenas on his penis when they rode into town on horseback.

He went to school, to which he had to travel on horseback. Although there were few books to read, Arenas's grandmother told him stories and made sure he went to school, and his mother taught him to write.

As economic conditions worsened, Arenas's grandfather sold the farm and moved the family into the town of Holguín. Once in town, Arenas, now thirteen, worked at a guava paste factory for twelve hours a day. On his day off, he went to the movies and tried to write novels, which he did in the evenings and at night and which, he later admitted, were dreadful. He went part-time to a junior high school where he dated girls, but his friends knew that he was gay, even though he himself had not accepted this yet.

When he was fourteen, Arenas decided to join the rebels. He traveled to where they were hiding, and they refused to let him join because they had enough men. However, when he arrived back home, his family had spread the news of his defection in the town, and Arenas had to flee back to the guerrillas for safety. They let him stay. He never saw any fighting, and he was still with the guerrillas when Batista fled from Cuba on December 31, 1958, and Fidel Castro took over. Arenas was now fifteen.

Arenas was given a scholarship to a new polytechnic institute where youths were trained to be agricultural accountants. The youths, and others like them, became the "vanguard of the revolution," the first Cubans indoctrinated into Castro's system. Arenas graduated in 1961 and was assigned to a farm near Manzanillo.

He used to go home to Holguín on weekends, and there he began an affair with a young man whom he met on the bus and discovered the homosexual subculture. Dissatisfied with the work on the farm, Arenas applied for and was accepted into a planning course at the University of Havana. Arenas still refused to accept that he was a homosexual, but a friend took him to the National Library where he met many homosexuals, and soon Arenas was cruising in Havana for lovers and pick-ups. He also switched from being the active sexual partner to being passive, a role he came to prefer.

In 1963, he entered a story in a competition at the National Library which so impressed the judges that they hired him. There he had much more time to write and to read. His book, Singing from the Well, won an award and was published, as was his second novel. However, when the head of the library changed and the regime became more oppressive, Arenas resigned his position at the library.

He associated with the other writers in Havana, and they would meet to read one another's works and discuss literature. Arenas also began to enter the homosexual subculture in earnest, even though the regime became more intolerant of homosexuality. By 1968, Arenas estimated, he had already had sex with some five thousand men. Arenas claimed that the sex was always free — there was no prostitution — and he noted that he liked strict roles in the sexual act, in which he was happiest being the passive partner. He was occasionally robbed and blackmailed in the course of his homosexual odyssey, but he remained undeterred.

He began working for the writers' union for which he had to check galley proofs, but at this time the harassment by the State Security increased. In 1967, he had met two visitors to Cuba, Jorge and Margarita Camacho, who kept in touch with Arenas after they left. He smuggled manuscripts out of the country with them which they helped publish abroad, and this met with further disapproval from the authorities.

In 1968, Castro sided with the Russians over their invasion of Czechoslovakia, confirming the repressive nature of his regime and destroying any faith Arenas and his friends had in the regime. Castro started ordering people to work in agriculture whenever this were needed. Arenas had to participate in the sugar cane harvest in 1970 after Castro had set an unreachable goal for the nation's harvest. The repression escalated. Writers were imprisoned and tortured until they recanted their opposition to the regime.

Arenas still visited his family in Holguín, but even his aunt had turned into a supporter of and agent for the regime, and she reported Arenas for his homosexuality and seditious writing. Although he continued to receive income from the writers' union, he was not allowed to write for them. In order to buy time, Arenas married a woman who wanted cover for her heterosexual affairs. In 1973, Arenas and a male lover had their possessions stolen by two young men with whom they had just had sex. They reported the theft, but the young men accused Arenas and his friend of being homosexuals. Arenas was charged with being a homosexual and a counterrevolutionary. Although he was arrested, the security at the police station was lax, and Arenas walked out that night. He made several attempts to escape, first by swimming to America and then, more reasonably, by trying to get to the American base at Guantanamo. The Cuban security was too tight, and Arenas had to return to Havana.

Arenas escaped capture for several months, but he was eventually captured and sent to the prison at Morro Castle. He tried to kill himself with an overdose of psychedelic drugs but he survived. He was placed in the cells for dangerous criminals, rather than those for homosexuals. He refused to have sex with anyone because sex under forced conditions was not enjoyable for Arenas, but his decision also helped keep him alive since he stayed out of the continual fights which centered around sex. When they were seeking Arenas, the police had spread the rumor that he was a rapist and murderer. This reputation helped him since the other prisoners were somewhat afraid of him.

After more than six months, Arenas was transferred to the State Security system where he was encouraged to confess his counterrevolutionary crimes and recant. After four months of isolation, Arenas confessed. He was then charged with corrupting minors and sentenced to two years in prison. He served this sentence at a open jail where the men were used to construct houses.

Just prior to his arrest, Arenas had caught syphilis. He had some treatment with penicillin, and after his release in 1976, he completed the treatment. He managed to pay a friend for an apartment by getting his aunt to give him money for never returning to the family house. He obtained money by a variety of means. A group of his friends found a furnished convent which had been boarded up. They stripped the convent, sold most of the contents and put the rest in their own apartments. He also sold clothes that his friends sent from abroad or which he purchased on the black market.

He continued to write, and he continued his homosexual life despite the dangers involved in both activities. In 1980, after Cubans stormed the Peruvian embassy in an effort to escape from Cuba, Castro decided to let some Cubans emigrate. He refused to let any important Cubans leave, but, in desperation, Arenas went to the local police station and presented himself as a common criminal who had been sentenced for a public disturbance. They gave him a permit for the Mariel exodus, and he left the port only hours before the authorities realized their mistake.

The boat he was on broke down and drifted. Instead of a trip of seven hours, they spent four days at sea before being rescued by the U.S. Coast Guard, but Arenas eventually reached freedom.

Life in America was not easy for Arenas. He did not like the Cubans in Florida and, when he began to write and speak out against Castro, his publishers refused to publish his works anymore. They also failed to pay him the royalties his books had earned.

In August 1980, he was invited to give a talk at Columbia University in New York, and, once there, he found that he loved New York. He found an apartment which he shared with a Cuban friend who had psychiatric problems and who had also escaped in the Mariel exodus. He was writing again, and he resumed his homosexual adventures. He worked against Castro, starting a magazine briefly and appearing in several anti-Castro films. By 1983, he had obtained a visa which enabled him to travel abroad. He went to Europe and met the Camachos who had helped him since 1967. His mother visited him, and he gave talks at some forty universities.

By the winter of 1987, Arenas was very sick and a doctor diagnosed him as having AIDS. By then, he had corrected most of the manuscripts he had smuggled out of Cuba, and he had written and published a number of other works. After a serious illness and three and a half months in hospital, Arenas returned to his apartment to find that someone had left him some rat poison, suggesting that he commit suicide. Arenas started dictating his autobiography into a tape recorder, since he was too weak to write. The French translation of The Doorman received a prize, and Arenas flew to Paris to receive it. But he soon came down with pneumonia and then cancer (Kaposi's sarcoma). But he survived again and began writing the fourth novel in his pentagoniá while revising the fifth, He came down with pneumonia again, and went to Spain to recover, where he helped write an open letter to Castro asking for free elections which was signed by thousands of people and published.

Suicide had always been a theme in Arenas's life. A great-uncle hung himself at home and, throughout his autobiography, he notes which friends, colleagues, notables and fellow prisoners committed suicide in Cuba. Indeed it seems from Arenas's autobiography that suicide was extremely common in Cuba. Arenas himself had made two previous attempts at suicide, when he was trying to escape from Cuba and when he was sent to prison in 1973.

As the illness worsened, his health deteriorated further, and his depression deepened. When he was no longer able to write, he decided to kill himself. He died of an overdose of drugs and alcohol on December 17, 1990, in Manhattan.

31. ROBERT CLIVE:

CONQUEROR OF INDIA

Richard Clive was a barrister and owned a country estate in Shropshire. He was a tyrant to his family and paid attention to his children only in order to punish them. To protect her first-born son, Robert, born September 29, 1725, from him, Rebecca Clive sent Robert to live with an uncle and aunt in Manchester when he was two years old. They had no children of their own and so welcomed the frail but difficult boy. Robert grew up to be aggressive and independent, with a fiery temper, and he was expelled from several schools. He led his gang in raids against shop keepers who refused to pay them "protection money." The only time that he was well-behaved was during a long and severe illness with a fever and convulsions.

Eventually, Robert's father decided that Robert, whom he called "that idiot," should be sent out of the country to India. Robert left England alone, without anyone seeing him off at the dock, to begin work as a clerk for the East India Company in Madras. He arrived there after fifteen months at sea on May 31, 1744.

At this time, the East India Company worked simply as a group of traders. The British government had no interest in making India a colony. When Clive arrived, there was great rivalry between the English and the French, with the Dutch playing a minor role.

At first Clive was miserable in India. He hated the work of a clerk, but he did not dare to return home. Most of the Europeans in India kept themselves apart from the Indians, except for visiting prostitutes, but Clive departed from this norm. He got involved with the Indians and learned their language.

Soon after his arrival, Clive underwent a medical

inspection and was found to have phimosis, a condition in which the foreskin constricts the penis. Against his will, Clive was circumcised. The later consequence of this was that Clive was more acceptable in Muslim high circles in India since all Muslim males were circumcised.

Clive worked as a clerk, joined his fellow Englishmen visiting the brothels of Madras, took opium pills to drug his consciousness and was desperately unhappy. One night, at the age of nineteen, alone in his room, he held his pistol to his head and pulled the trigger twice. The gun failed to fire. His friend, Edmund Maskelyne, came by, and Clive asked him to fire the gun out of the window. The gun discharged. Clive decided that he was meant to live and thereafter changed his life style. He spent his free time in the library of the Governor of Madras, reading the books there, and he learned Hindustani and Persian.

India was at that time ruled by the Grand Mughal, a descendent of the Mongol conquerors of India, but the country had split up into smaller regions, each ruled by a local dictator. This gave the British and the French an opportunity for conquest, for the Hindus preferred the Europeans as rulers rather than the Muslim usurpers.

The major French region on the west coast of India was at Pondicherry, governed by Joseph-Francois Dupleix. When the War of the Austrian Succession broke out, England and France went to war, and Dupleix was ordered to capture Madras. The French attacked on September 14, 1746. The English soon surrendered, but Clive and some friends slipped out of the town disguised as Muslim mercantile agents. It took them eight days to reach Pondicherry, where they found the Governor of Madras chained, stripped naked and paraded through the streets.

Twenty miles south of Pondicherry lay the English fort St. David. Clive and his friends went there and helped defend it during a three month siege by Dupleix. Clive loved the fighting, and eventually the French were repulsed. Clive fought so well that he was appointed as an ensign, or sub-lieutenant, of the Second Company of European Volunteer Foot Soldiers of Fort David.

After reinforcements arrived from England, the English under Major Stringer Lawrence, attacked Pondicherry, but failed to take it. In 1748, the war ended in Europe, and so the warring factions in India had to call a halt to their fighting.

In 1749, Lawrence decided to attack the fort of Devikota south of Fort St. David in order to restore the deposed Rajah to the throne. Lieutenant Clive was Lawrence's personal aide. Clive led the charge, with 35 Europeans and seven hundred natives. Only four of the Europeans survived, but Clive was one of them, and Devikota surrendered.

It is important to note that Clive always led his men into battle, and, though soldiers standing at his side were often killed, he was rarely wounded. His seeming "immortality" combined with his phenomenal success in battles led the Muslims and Hindus of India to regard him with awe. After these experiences, Clive decided not to return to work as a clerk but stayed with the army. He was promoted to Captain, and his friend Maskelyne was appointed as an ensign and Clive's aide. Clive came down with malaria and dengue fever in 1750 but recovered on opium and quinine.

Dupleix immediately began allying himself with some of the local rulers in order to defeat others, trying to build up a greater region of influence for the French. The English followed suit, but Dupleix soon controlled most of southern India. Meanwhile, Clive rose in rank, becoming the commissariat chief, and he was made a junior merchant, allowing him to trade privately. He soon had a fortune of forty thousands pounds.

The first English expeditions against the French

failed, as Clive foresaw they would. Given more freedom, Clive first reinforced Trichinopoly, then led an expedition against Arcot. Although Clive was outnumbered two to one, the defenders fled. Clive took the town without a shot being fired, and he forbad looting and brutalizing the inhabitants, which won him support from the residents of the town. The French along with Chanda Sahib, the Governor of Trichinopoly, sent 7000 Hindustani soldiers and 150 Frenchmen to attack Arcot. They took the town, but could not take the fort, manned by only eighty Europeans and 120 Indians. Clive was ill with malaria and out of opium, and he had only laudanum and quinine to take. Despite his illness, when the Indians attacked, Clive decimated them with his battery and the determined fighting of his men. The horde fled, leaving the English with only four killed and two wounded. Clive followed this success with a defeat of 400 French and 4500 Indians with his own army of 380 English and 1300 Indians. It was now clear to the native leaders that the English would be better partners than the French. Clive himself was recognized as Kampeni Jehan Behadur, The Greatly Daring In War. After these battles, Indians and many Europeans refused to serve under any captain but Clive.

Lawrence arrived back in India in 1752, and he was wise enough to make Clive his second-in-command despite Clive's low rank, telling his disgruntled officers that Clive was a military genius. Lawrence and Clive then relieved the English under siege at Trichinopoly — 1,500 soldiers defeated an enemy army of 23,000.

After this, Clive was again ill with fever and fatigue and the effects of wounds received in the battles. His friend, Maskelyne, had sent for his sixteen year-old sister to come to India. When Peggy arrived, she and Clive fell in love at once. They were married on February 18, 1753. It should be mentioned here that Clive appears to have been hypersexual for most of his life. He masturbated constantly, and he engaged in oral and anal sex with both men and women. Part of this was a consequence of the mores of the time in India where indiscriminate sexual behavior was the norm for everyone, European or Indian. However, even allowing for the general promiscuous sexual behavior, Clive seems to have been especially active. Despite this, he appears to have loved his wife dearly, and she was continually pregnant, though some of the pregnancies ended in miscarriages. Clive did not abstain from his sexual activities upon marrying Peggy, but he did give up drugs.

Soon after the wedding, Clive was ill with epileptoid convulsions, and he was given a leave so that he could return to England. Back in London, he was the social lion of the season. The press hailed his victories, the titled sought him as a guest for their parties, and the politicians sought his advice. Clive and Peggy lived in Queen's Square off St. James's Place.

Clive decided to stand for parliament and, though he apparently won, was unseated in a new election because of the enmity of the Prime Minister. Saddened by this defeat, Clive asked to return to India, and he came back as Lieutenant-Colonel of Foot in India.

Clive was soon involved in the petty wars again, but he then met the major challenge of his career, the battle that won India for the English. A young ruler, Sirajuddawleh, in Bengal was especially savage and desirous of power. As a child he tortured his pets and sodomised his playmates. As an adolescent, he was a paranoid sadist. He decided to conquer the rival forces in Bengal, and he led an army of 40,000 against Fort William, adjacent to Calcutta, and defeated the English there. He then put 146 European captives into a dungeon, eighteen feet by fifteen feet — the "Black Hole of Calcutta." The next day only 23 were still alive. The 21 men who survived were circumcised and set free after several weeks of rape by Sirajuddawleh's soldiers.

The English knew that Clive was needed. So on October 1756, Clive set sail from Madras to Calcutta. Meanwhile, the English and French were again at war, this time in North America, ending the truce in India. On January 3, 1757, Colonel Clive (on behalf of the East India Company) and Admiral Watson on behalf of the Crown declared war on Sirajuddawleh. In the first battle, Clive, with 800 Europeans and 1500 Indians, defeated the enemy forces of 15,000 foot soldiers and 18,000 horsemen. Although Sirajuddawleh signed a treaty with the English after this, he continued to plot against them.

Clive defeated the French at Chandernagore in March, and soon after had to face Sirajuddawleh again. Despite Clive's efforts to avert a battle by negotiation, the two opposing armies met up at Plassey. Clive had 1000 Europeans, 100 Eurasians, and 2100 Indians. Sirajuddawleh had some 100,000 men entrenched at Plassey. Clive was outnumbered thirty to one. Clive's anxiety before the battle drove him to sexual excess. His servants observed him masturbating, were ordered to perform fellatio on him, and procured a camp whore for him.

The battle took place on June 23, 1757. Clive's allies failed to appear, and none of the other leaders in Bengal had given any sign that they would leave Sirajuddawleh's army and support Clive. Clive had to attack alone. By 5 pm the battle was over. Clive lost 24 killed and 48 wounded. The enemy lost 600 men, and the rest fled. Not only did this battle secure India for the English, it brought Bengali gold pouring into England, which stimulated English industry and made London the capitalist leader of the world, thereby facilitating the industrial revolution.

But what was Clive to do with his reluctant allies? He made the chief of them, Mir Ja'fer, Viceroy of Bengal, but Clive made it clear that Mir Ja'fer was simply a puppet.

Sirajuddawleh tried to flee but was captured and put to death by Mir Ja'fer's son. Robert Clive, aged thirty-one, was master of Bengal. All over India he was now Bare Jangi-Lat Sahib Behadur — the Great and Bold Warlord Sahib.

Again, Clive did not plunder the land, nor brutalize the Indians. He even returned gifts from the local leaders. In this way, he won their trust and devotion as well as their fear and respect. Although there were plots on his life, he had supporters who thwarted these plots.

Of course Clive was a good businessman, and he did not go poor. He gave gifts to his five sisters, his parents and more distant relatives, his in-laws, and even Colonel Lawrence who had given Clive the chance to show what a fine soldier he was.

Clive wanted to return to England as soon as possible, but the commander-in-chief of the English forces, Admiral Charles Watson, died in August. Although the East India Company named four co-governors of Bengal, all four resigned in favor of Clive. Thus, despite his continuing malarial fever, eased only a little by quinine and opium, and his temperament (an inherent melancholia interspersed with fits of anxiety and overwork), Clive stayed on from 1758 to 1760 to govern, taking care to increase his wealth. Clive reorganized the administration of the territories, and at the same time obtained a gift of land (twenty-four fertile districts adjoining Calcutta) from the Viceroy of Bengal which would provide him with an untaxed annual income of one million rupees. The English eliminated the remaining French interests in India, and followed this up by eliminating the Dutch. Meanwhile, enmity toward Clive grew among the London directors of the East India Company, particularly Laurence Sulivan, the Chairman.

Clive and his family sailed for England on February 21, 1760. His second homecoming outshone his first. He was hailed as a conquering hero and a great statesman, and he was also the richest person in Great Britain. King George, now growing madder by the year, awarded Clive the Order of the Bath, but not an English title, and so Clive purchased an Irish estate which made him Baron of Plassey in the Kingdom of Ireland. His efforts to get into the House of Commons still aroused a great deal of opposition, but he won a seat in April 1761.

Meanwhile, his enemy, Sulivan, had won back control of the East India Company. Then in 1764 word reached England that the new Viceroy of Bengal had executed about two hundred Europeans in Patna and had the three leaders decapitated and castrated. The East India Company requested Clive to return to India to restore order, but he declined. After a brief battle of wills, Sulivan had to admit defeat. Sulivan was replaced by Charles Rouse, a supporter of Clive, and Clive agreed to return to India.

Clive left England on June 4, 1764, landed in India on April 10, 1766, and began to clean up the mess. He negotiated to annex all of Bengal into official Company control. He also allowed the Indians to collect the taxes, leaving the English to dispose of them, thereby allowing each group to share in the administration of government. But Clive's physical and mental disorders continued to plague him. He suffered from fevers and fits of melancholia to such an extent that his aides had to tie him to the bed to prevent him from doing harm to himself. He left India for the last time in January 1767.

Clive returned home to his palatial home in Berkeley Square and to further honors, even being acclaimed in Paris despite the fact that he had defeated the French. According to reports at the time, Clive seduced (or was seduced by) large numbers of women while touring Europe.

Returning to London in 1768, Clive found growing opposition to him both in Parliament and the Company.

Pamphlets were written attacking Clive, and his supporters published defenses. Eventually, in April 1772, the House of Commons appointed a committee to look into the affairs of the East India Company in India, but the committee quickly turned to an examination of Clive's behavior. Finally, a motion was presented to censure Clive. Clive's supporters managed to get the most condemnatory passages deleted, and they added amendments asserting that Clive had rendered "great and meritorious services to his country." Thus, the motion, as passed in May 1773, absolved Clive of all guilt.

Despite the victory, Clive fell into great despondency. He shut himself off from his family and friends for days at a time. The months of anguish and anxiety had taken its toll. His mental condition was exacerbated by an attack of gallstones which was excruciatingly painful. Drugs (primarily laudanum) helped the pain a little, but failed to relieve his depression. His conditioned worsened, until on November 22, 1774, he took all of the opium at his disposal and died.

32. EDWIN HOWARD ARMSTRONG:

THE INVENTOR OF RADIO

Edwin Howard Armstrong was an inventor who held the patents for two of the major advances in this century which led to the development of radio. He was born on December 18, 1890, in the Chelsea district of Manhattan. His father, John, worked for the Oxford University Press, and his mother, Emily, came from a prominent business family in the city. She was a graduate of Hunter College and taught in the public schools for ten years before marrying John. The family moved several times, eventually ending up in Yonkers.

Armstrong, the first-born, went to the public schools where he was a good student. When he was nine, he came down with St. Vitus' Dance which causes involuntary twitchings and movements. Armstrong was kept home for two years, nursed by his mother and tutored by a great-aunt. He recovered with only a slight tic noticeable for the rest of his life — hitching his shoulder forward and twisting his neck.

After this illness, Armstrong became even more thoughtful and withdrawn. He had always been interested in mechanical toys, and his social introversion led him to spend even more time with this hobby. In 1904, his father brought him back from England The Boys' Book Of Inventions, and Armstrong decided to become an inventor. As soon as he entered high school, his interests focused on wireless, and he was particularly enamored of Michael Faraday who had discovered electrical induction (the principle of the dynamo) and Guglielmo Marconi who was the first to transmit radio signals. Armstrong commandeered the attic and filled it with his equipment. The family nicknamed him Buzz, and he soon found others in the neighborhood fascinated by the new inventions, including a retired engineer from the old American Telegraph Company. In 1910, Armstrong built his own permanent antenna 125 feet high in the backyard, helped by his younger sister. Despite (or maybe because of) his hobby, he was judged to be only a fair student at high school. He took up tennis as a sport and became captain of the high school team. He graduated in 1909 and entered the department of engineering at Columbia University.

Armstrong graduated from Columbia, but his path was unorthodox. He puttered in the laboratory at all hours and tended to focus on his own interests rather than course assignments. Several faculty complained about him, but he had won the support of several influential faculty members who protected him. He spent most of his time in his attic or in the laboratory at Columbia and, in his junior year, he solved the problem of regenerative receiver circuits. He wanted to file for a patent, but his father refused to loan him the money ($150) until he graduated. He was unable to raise the money himself, and so he recorded his invention on paper and had it notarized — on January 31, 1913.

Armstrong graduated in June 1913, and he was offered an appointment as an assistant in the department for one year for $600 a year. His father loaned him the money for the patent which was filed on October 29, 1913, with an addition on December 18. (The patent was issued on October 6, 1914.) Radio engineers were impressed by the demonstrations of his circuits (sending and receiving radio signals over long distances), and one of those who came to see them was David Sarnoff, later to become head of RCA and one of Armstrong's bitter enemies. Another engineer who came to see the invention was Lee de Forest who later challenged the primacy of Armstrong's patent (and won in the United States Supreme Court). Armstrong published a report of his work in Electrical World in December, 1914.

In 1914, three rivals filed patents on the invention, including de Forest, Armstrong's father died of a stroke in 1915, and now Armstrong was the sole provider for the family (his mother and two sisters). Licences for his invention were bringing in only $100 a month, and efforts to sell the rights to his invention came to nought as the major companies involved tried to see if they could develop alternatives in their laboratories to circumvent the patents. AT&T bought up rival patents, including de Forest's interfering patents. However, the amateur community recognized Armstrong's importance, even if industry refused to, by electing him President of the Radio Club of America in 1916.

By 1916, however, Armstrong's situation eased. The American Marconi Company realized the utility of Armstrong's patent and bought a licence, thereafter paying him about $500 a month in royalties. Then in 1917, America entered the Great War.

The First World War halted Armstrong's efforts to some extent. He joined the army as a captain, and was posted to Europe (headquartered in Paris) and given the task of organizing the communication systems for the military. He made several good friends who later worked with him back in America, and he had time to work on more inventions, in particular the superheterodyne circuit. After the armistice was signed, he filed for a patent (February 8, 1919) which was issued on June 8, 1920, another historic milestone in radio.

In 1919, he was promoted to Major, and he received the Chevalier de la Légion d'honneur from the French. He had also been awarded the first Medal of Honor from the Institute of Radio Engineers in America. He arrived back home in September 1919. Back in America, Armstrong returned to work at Columbia University, fought the rival patent suit from de Forest and worked on the development of the superheterodyne. Again rival patents were filed and suits brought.

In the twenties, Armstrong sold two inventions for a large sum, won an initial victory over de Forest in federal court, came up with a third invention which he sold for an even larger sum. The money came to Armstrong from Westinghouse which had been left out by General Electric and AT&T and now wanted to get into the game. Although Armstrong had to pay large sum to the lawyers acting on his behalf in the patent suits, he still had a healthy income. At the same time, amateur radio began to boom, and Armstrong's lawyers advised him to license his inventions for amateur use (in crystal-detector sets), and royalties poured in from this source too. In 1922, his monthly income rose to $10,000.

Now that radio stations were opening in cities across America, the amateur inventors moved to shortwave signals. With Armstrong helping, a group managed to send shortwave messages across the Atlantic in 1921. Although Sarnoff and his aides from RCA came to watch, the industry did not see the value of this invention until 1927. Again, the amateurs were in the forefront of developments, not industry.

Meanwhile, Armstrong had discovered the super-regenerative circuit, a patent for which was issued in July, 1922. RCA finally came to terms with Armstrong and bought his superregenerative circuit for $200,000 cash and 60,000 shares of RCA stock, making him the largest individual stockholder. Later patents that year netted him 20,000 more shares, and made him a millionaire. Furthermore, he invested well and avoided losses in the stock market crash later.

In his dealings with RCA, Armstrong had met Sarnoff's secretary, and in 1922 he asked her out. Marion MacInnis was twenty-two, of Scottish descent, and from New England. After a quick romance, they married on December 1st, 1922.

Armstrong was appointed as an Assistant Professor at Columbia University, but he refused to accept any salary, taught no classes, and gave only occasional lectures.

De Forest, backed by AT&T, had not given up after his first loss in federal court, and the ensuing court battles lasted from 1920 to 1924 costing close to a million dollars in legal fees. De Forest tried to establish priority to the invention, and Armstrong fought, not because of the royalties involved, for he was already a millionaire, but because of the principle. He had invented the regenerative receiver circuit, radio engineers knew it, but the courts were not sure. At the initial victory in 1922 by Armstrong, he should have accepted or waived damages so that the case could be closed, but Armstrong would not allow Westinghouse (his supporter in the court battles) to waive damages, and he would not allow de Forest a compromise in which de Forest would purchase a company already licensed by Westinghouse. Given this breathing space, and a sign of Armstrong's intransigence, de Forest pressed on in his suits and began to win. By 1927, all of the court verdicts were in de Forest's favor, and in 1928 the United States Supreme Court upheld the judgments in favor of de Forest. Armstrong did not give up, but came to the support of a small company sued by RCA and backed its fight up to the Supreme Court again, where in 1934, the court again supported de Forest. AT&T benefitted from this since Armstrong's patents ran out in 1931, after which no royalties would be due, whereas de Forest's patents filed much later ran through 1941. Thus Armstrong and de Forest were pawns in a much larger fight between rival corporations, but the suits were made more complicated by the personality of both Armstrong and de Forest who wanted legal confirmation of their inventions. Armstrong was, however, the major inventor, and only his vanity prevented an early and compromise settlement back in 1922.

In 1934, Armstrong attended the annual convention of the Institute of Radio Engineers. He had informed the Institute that he would return the medal awarded him in 1918 for the invention which the United States Supreme Court now said was de Forest's. He was not given the opportunity. The Institute's president addressed him from the chair and affirmed the earlier award and his precedence as inventor of the regenerative circuit. The meeting gave him a standing ovation, and the board which had unanimously agreed to this had many members employed by AT&T and RCA which had fought Armstrong and won in court!

Despite this, industry representatives and publications continued for many years to downplay the role of Armstrong and to promote the name of de Forest as the inventor of the regenerative circuit.

During these legal battles, Armstrong continued to invent and to enjoy life a little. He played tennis, vacationed with his wife, and spent summers at the Long Island beaches. He also continued to work on the problems of radio, and he now made an even more important discovery. In late 1933, he was issued patents for a new radio signaling system, later developed as FM radio, which solved the problem of atmospheric disturbances (static) which plagued AM radio. Although the laboratories of the major corporations had dabbled in this area, they had concluded that FM signaling was impossible. Armstrong's invention led to the revision of a "law" in the field, called Hartley's Law (named after an AT&T scientist).

The professor of the department at Columbia University (Michael Pupin), long a supporter of Armstrong, died in 1935. Armstrong was appointed as head of the Marcellus Hartley Research Laboratory in his place, at a nominal salary of $1 a year. Armstrong supplied the equipment, paid the assistants, and paid the overhead expenses.

Armstrong demonstrated his FM system publicly in late 1935 and, though the quality of sound was impressive, the radio industry (now organized into NBC, CBS, ABC, and the Mutual Broadcasting System) was reluctant to adopt it. They had invested a great deal of money and effort in AM radio, and they did not see the sense in setting up a rival system. Thus, in public and before congress and regulatory agencies (the FCC had been established in 1927 and reorganized in 1934), the industry continued to attack FM signaling and to hinder its development. At the same time, RCA began to set its own engineers to work up their own patents and to engage in interference proceedings in the Patent Office against Armstrong's patents. Undaunted, of course, Armstrong decided to invest his own money in setting up FM radio stations.

He obtained a license to operate in the small range of frequencies allotted by the FCC (2.7 megacycles versus the 120 megacycles allotted for experimental television), and he set out to build a 50-kilowatt station at Alpine, New Jersey, high on the Palisades overlooking the Hudson River. Armstrong's mother died in 1938, as the station was being built. Soon others were building FM stations elsewhere in America (Worcester and Hartford were the first). Armstrong's station opened in 1939, having cost $300,000, and the quality of its broadcasts was outstanding.

In 1939, the dam broke, and General Electric came out for FM. RCA at first fought the FM industry at the FCC, trying to limit FM's place in the spectrum of frequencies, but in 1940 it lost. RCA then decided to support FM, and Sarnoff tried to purchase the rights to Armstrong's patent for a lump sum. Armstrong again behaved stubbornly. He refused, demanding the royalties other companies paid. RCA refused Armstrong's terms.

The Armstrongs lived in a nice apartment in Manhattan, and they now bought a house at Rye Beach in New Hampshire. The Second World War meant an end to the expansion of FM radio, and a large decrease in the royalty payments to Armstrong. However, Armstrong let the military use his inventions without charge. Armstrong had already been advising the Signal Corps, and soon all of the military was using FM for communications. Armstrong also worked on a novel form of radar, and at the end of the war was awarded the United States Medal for Merit.

Once the war ended, FM radio took off again, and the battle resumed between the industry and the FM radio operators. The nascent television industry needed wavelengths assigned in the FM region, and so the FCC sided with industry and moved the FM radio stations from the 50 megacycle band to a new band between 88 and 108 megacycles for which they did not have the equipment. FM stations were also restricted by the FCC in power so that each station could serve only one small region. Despite this, the FM stations prospered, after a period of adjustment, and Armstrong's royalties poured in, despite the fact that companies like RCA refused to pay him royalties even they were using his inventions. Armstrong, himself, refused to reduce his fees although, by doing so, companies like RCA might have paid them. Furthermore, Armstrong had spent close to $1 million on his Alpine station, and he supported several other groups and organizations. Thus, his money was being spent as quickly as it arrived.

Eventually RCA decided to challenge Armstrong's patents in court. By doing so, they not only challenged Armstrong's pride as the inventor, they also tied him up in costly litigation. In 1948, the patents for FM had only two more years to run (after which the royalties would dry up), and the court battle began in earnest. He filed suit against RCA on July 22, 1948, seeking to get triple damages for the equipment made illegally by RCA during the term of his patents.

The battle lasted five years and ended with Armstrong's suicide. Most of the five years was taken up with depositions, but Armstrong also wrote scores of articles and letters to newspapers and magazines correcting the history of the development of radio which often ignored or minimized his own role. There were several attempts at a settlement, but Armstrong wanted vindication, which for him meant victory in court.

Inevitably, his marriage suffered. Marion had learned to live with his passion for radio. She had made a life for herself, without children, but often lonely. Now the court case consumed more and more of Armstrong's time, their money was being used up rapidly, and Armstrong himself looked close to having a breakdown. The crisis came in November 1953, at Thanksgiving when, after a row, Marion left to stay with her widowed sister. Armstrong's financial state was now in precarious. RCA made one last effort at a settlement, amounting to $2 million, but Armstrong rejected this. Armstrong's despondency grew.

On the night of January 31, 1954, Armstrong wrote a letter to his wife, dressed warmly in his overcoat, hat, scarf and gloves, and jumped from the thirteenth floor of his apartment building to his death.

David Sarnoff, head of RCA, attended the funeral, and RCA paid Armstrong's estate one million dollars to settle the suit. Too little, too late!

REFLECTIONS

One of the more immediate thoughts after reading about the lives of these suicides is that they are a very heterogeneous group. If we were hoping to find a "suicidal profile," we would fail. It is hard to see what, if anything, people as diverse as Alan Turing, Konoe Fumimaro and Robert Clive have in common. It is difficult even to find groups or "clusters" of similar suicides, so that we could describe three or four possible profiles into which we could classify the suicides. However, some generalizations are possible from this sample of suicides.

Suicide does not generally run in families. Leicester Hemingway, the younger brother of Ernest Hemingway, did have a father and two siblings commit suicide, but it is more likely that a psychiatric disorder, probably a depressive disorder, was inherited in this family and that this psychiatric disorder increased the probability of suicide in the descendants of Leicester Hemingway's father. Apart from the Hemingways, only Kenneth Halliwell, the murderer of Joe Orton, and Willard Hershberger, the baseball player, had a parent commit suicide.

One major factor present in many suicides is psychiatric illness. Many of the suicides described in this book did indeed have a psychiatric illness. The particular psychiatric disorder which best describes Vincent Van Gogh is still debated. Was it epilepsy, a personality disorder, or a schizophrenic psychosis? It is hard to say without the benefits of a modern clinical interview. But depression was clearly present in many of the suicides, including Arshille Gorky, Paul Kammerer, and Marilyn Monroe; and depression severe enough to be considered a psychiatric illness was present in others, such as Abbie Hoffman and Anne

Sexton. Interestingly, few of these suicides appear to be grossly psychotic (with the exception of James Forrestal), but that may be because this is a sample of famous suicides. People with schizophrenia may be less likely to achieve much in our society so that, although they may commit suicide at a higher rate than the average citizen, they are less likely to appear in this sample.

Those who abuse alcohol and drugs have a much higher rate of suicide, and many of the suicides here were substances abusers, including Elvis Presley, Judy Garland, Marilyn Monroe, and Brian Epstein. Substance abuse is seen by some commentators as a form of suicide since it reduces your life expectancy. It has been called <u>chronic suicide</u> since it kills you slowly over a long period of time. Thus, it is not surprising that substance abusers sometimes decide to kill themselves more quickly by suicide.

Loss, especially of a parent, is common in the sample. In a published study of a slightly different sample of famous suicides, I found that exactly half had lost a parent or parent substitute or had a very disruptive childhood, and the loss was most commonly experienced between the ages of six and sixteen, a period which, according to classical psychoanalysis, not much of interest happens to shape our lives. In the present sample, there were many examples, including Leicester Hemingway who, only thirteen years old, was at home when his father shot himself. Kenneth Halliwell was eleven when his mother died from a wasp sting. and Judy Garland was thirteen when her father died. Arshille Gorky's father left the family when Arshille was four, and Arshille's mother died of starvation in his arms when he was fifteen!

Some of the suicides had disrupted childhoods. Marilyn Monroe was placed with a number of foster families, and her mother entered and left Marilyn's life unpredictably. Children need a safe and predictable world in order to become psychologically healthy, and Marilyn's childhood was far from ideal. Robert Clive, too, was sent away to live with relatives, while Mark Rothko's father left the family in Latvia to come to America, sending for his wife and children when Mark was ten.

The effect of age is interesting. First, the suicides of the younger people do "make as much sense" as those of the older individuals. The young people do not seem to have experienced sufficient stressors to make them suicidal, whereas the older people have an overabundance of stressors. In the present sample, Freddie Prinze killed himself at the age of twenty-two after singing at President Kennedy's inaugural ball. He was a star on the way up, and a broken marriage does not seem to be sufficient as a precipitating event. On the other hand, we look at Charles Boyer, whose only child committed suicide and whose wife died, leaving Boyer alone at the age of seventy-nine. He killed himself two days after his wife died. That seems to be a more rational suicide.

Some of the suicides seem especially troublesome because they seem so "unfair." Alan Turing was persecuted for being a homosexual and killed himself in 1954, and we know that homosexuality was decriminalized in England in the early 1960s. Vincent Van Gogh never sold a painting during his life, and now his glorious paintings sell for obscene sums of money from which he gains no benefit. If only David Sarnoff, the head of RCA, had given Edwin Armstrong the one million dollars before his suicide instead of giving it to his estate afterwards. Mrs. Koestler and Mrs. Zweig killed themselves because their husbands wanted to die, whereas we would have tried to persuade them that they would be better off without their depressed and domineering husbands.

Yet others cause us concern because, as we read them, we ask ourselves, "How would I cope with such a crisis? Could I find the will to go on, or would I kill myself as this person did?" Each of us has our own reasons for thinking about suicide. Some commit suicide to avoid becoming mentally ill, while others become mentally ill to avoid killing themselves. Some people kill themselves as a political protest, burning themselves in public as some Buddhist monks did in Vietnam during their war, while others think that such a choice is irrational.

For me, the suicides of Charles Boyer and Sigmund Freud raise concern. I am getting old, and I wonder how I would handle the loss of my wife in my old age or a terribly painful medical illness. Freud, ahead of his time as usual, arranged for a physician-assisted suicide, an option that is being discussed in many nations these days. I want that option available for me too. How would I handle the prospect of a long psychiatric illness (James Forrestal) or a life in prison (Konoe Fumimaro if they did not execute him).

And how would I kill myself? Would I use a gun like Freddie Prinze or jump from a building like Edwin Armstrong? I think not. Perhaps an overdose of barbiturates like Charles Boyer. As I get older, the suicides I identify with change. In my earlier years, the break-up of a marriage and years of living alone seemed to be a major stressor, but I survived those life events. Now happily married, I anticipate the problems of retirement and old age.

One final note. All of the people whose lives are described in this book achieved fame. All are remembered. Indeed you have just read about them in this book, although they most likely do not gain any satisfaction from that. Most suicides, however, are not famous. They live ordinary, drab lives. They kill themselves, and no one writes a biography of them. Yet their lives are filled with as much as pain as these artists, scientists, film stars, and leaders. Let us not forget them. They deserve a moment of silence too.

BIBLIOGRAPHY

This book was made possible by the autobiographies and biographies of the these suicides. Here are the references for those I used.

Abrahamsen S. *The mind and death of a genius.* New York: Columbia University Press, 1946.

Allday, E. *Stefan Zweig.* Chicago: J. Philip O'Hara, 1972.

Arenas, R. *Before night falls.* New York: Viking, 1993.

Barbour, J. *The death of Willard Hershberger.* The National Pastime, 1987, 6(1), 62-65.

Blue, A. *Who was "Mrs. Arthur Koestler" and why did she kill herself?* Ms Magazine, 1983, 12(1), 110.

Canetto, S. S. *She died for love and he for glory.* Omega, 1992-1993, 26, 1-17.

Coleman, R. *The man who made the Beatles.* New York: McGraw-Hill, 1989.

Demaris, O. *Brothers in blood.* New York: Scribners, 1977.

Edwardes, A. *The rape of India.* New York: Julian, 1966.

Eells, G. *Final Gig.* San Diego: Harcourt Brace Jovanovich, 1991.

Frank, G. *Judy.* New York: Harper & Row, 1975.

Gay, P. *Freud.* New York: Norton, 1988.

Goldman, A. *Elvis.* New York: McGraw-Hill, 1981.

Goldman, A. *Down at the end of lonely street.* Life, 1990, 13(8), 96-104.

Guiles, F. L. *Legend.* New York: Stein & Day, 1984.

Hemingway, L. *My brother, Ernest Hemingway.* Cleveland: World, 1961.

Hodges, A. *Alan Turing.* New York: Simon & Schuster, 1983.

Honour, A. *Tormented genius.* New York: Morrow, 1967.

Hughes-Hallett, L. *Cleopatra.* New York: Harper Collins, 1990.

Jezer, M. *Abbie Hoffman.* New Brunswick, NJ: Rutgers University Press, 1992.

Koestler, A. *The case of the midwife toad.* New York: Random House, 1971.

Lahr, J. *Prick up your ears.* New York: Knopf, 1978.

Lane, A. J. *To Herland and beyond.* New York: Pantheon, 1990.

Lessing, L. *Man of high fidelity.* Philadelphia: Lippincott, 1956.

Lester, D., & Topp, R. *Suicide in the major leagues.* Perceptual and Motor Skills, 1988, 67, 934.

Levene, M. *Arthur Koestler.* New York: Frederick Ungar, 1984.

Linet, B. *Ladd.* New York: Arbor House, 1979.

McVay, G. *Isadora and Esenin.* Ann Arbor, MI: Ardis, 1980.

Meyers, J. *Hemingway.* New York: Harper & Row, 1985.

Middlebrook, D. W. *Anne Sexton.* Boston: Houghton-Mifflin, 1991.

Mikes, G. *Remembering the Koestlers.* American Scholar, 1984, 53, 219-224.

Mooradian, K. *The many worlds of Arshile Gorky.* Chicago: Gilgamesh, 1980.

Oka, Y. *Konoe Fumimaro.* Tokyo University Press, 1983.

Prater, D. A. <u>European of yesteryear.</u> Oxford: Oxford University Press, 1972.

Pruetzel, M. *The Freddie Prinze story.* Kalamazoo, MI: Master's Press, 1978.

Rogow, A. A. *James Forrestal.* New York: Macmillan.

Seldes, L. *The legacy of Mark Rothko.* New York: Holt, Rinehart & Winston, 1978.

Stone, I. F. *The trial of Socrates.* Boston: Little Brown, 1988.

Swindell, L. *Charles Boyer.* Garden City, NY: Doubleday, 1983.

Voss, R. F. *William Inge.* In J. MacNicholas (Ed.) Dictionary of Literary Biography, Volume 7. Detroit: Gale Research Company, 1981, 325-337.

Wickett, A. *Double exit.* Eugene, OR: Hemlock Society, 1989.